CHEATING CHEATERS

A COMEDY BY
JOHN PATRICK

DRAMATISTS
PLAY SERVICE
INC.

CHEATING CHEATERS
Copyright © 1985, John Patrick
Copyright © 1983, John Patrick
as an unpublished dramatic composition

All Rights Reserved

CAUTION: Professionals and amateurs are hereby warned that performance of CHEATING CHEATERS is subject to payment of a royalty. It is fully protected under the copyright laws of the United States of America, and of all countries covered by the International Copyright Union (including the Dominion of Canada and the rest of the British Commonwealth), and of all countries covered by the Pan-American Copyright Convention, the Universal Copyright Convention, the Berne Convention, and of all countries with which the United States has reciprocal copyright relations. All rights, including without limitation professional/amateur stage rights, motion picture, recitation, lecturing, public reading, radio broadcasting, television, video or sound recording, all other forms of mechanical, electronic and digital reproduction, transmission and distribution, such as CD, DVD, the Internet, private and file-sharing networks, information storage and retrieval systems, photocopying, and the rights of translation into foreign languages are strictly reserved. Particular emphasis is placed upon the matter of readings, permission for which must be secured from the Author's agent in writing.

The English language stock and amateur stage performance rights in the United States, its territories, possessions and Canada for CHEATING CHEATERS are controlled exclusively by DRAMATISTS PLAY SERVICE, INC., 440 Park Avenue South, New York, NY 10016. No professional or nonprofessional performance of the Play may be given without obtaining in advance the written permission of DRAMATISTS PLAY SERVICE, INC., and paying the requisite fee.

Inquiries concerning all other rights should be addressed to Dramatists Play Service, Inc., 440 Park Avenue South, New York, NY 10016.

SPECIAL NOTE
Anyone receiving permission to produce CHEATING CHEATERS is required to give credit to the Author as sole and exclusive Author of the Play on the title page of all programs distributed in connection with performances of the Play and in all instances in which the title of the Play appears for purposes of advertising, publicizing or otherwise exploiting the Play and/or a production thereof. The name of the Author must appear on a separate line, in which no other name appears, immediately beneath the title and in size of type equal to 50% of the size of the largest, most prominent letter used for the title of the Play. No person, firm or entity may receive credit larger or more prominent than that accorded the Author.

CAST

THERESA — *The first nun — sweet and scatterbrained.*

ANGELICA — *The second nun — gracious and intelligent.*

BENJAMIN — *An inventive young man — attractive and audacious.*

BOZO — *A police officer, lowest rank — fourth grade elementary education.*

TANIA — *An art student — young and beguiling.*

CHEATING CHEATERS

ACT I

TIME — The present.

PLACE — A modest living room in an old apartment building.

AT RISE — There is no one onstage as curtain rises. An entrance door is Stage Left and opposite on the Right is a door to the kitchen. Doors to bedrooms are Upstage Center. There is a skylight above a center table. After a moment of adjustments the hall door opens and Theresa, a diminutive nun in a traditional black habit, enters carrying a folding stool, a red pot, and a sign reading: "God Loveth A Cheerful Giver."

THERESA. Angelica? *(Waits.)* Angelica! *(She beams happily and puts her "accouterments" on the table. She then takes a chair and places it under the bookshelves. She mounts it and removes a book. She takes out a hidden bottle of bourbon and reads the label in joyous anticipation. Behind her, Angelica, another nun, enters unobserved. She also carries a stool, a red pot, and a sign reading: "It Is Later Than You Think." She puts these down and tiptoes up to stand behind Theresa.)*
ANGELICA. *(As Theresa takes a swallow.)* Theresa! *(Theresa sprays out a mouthful of bourbon.)*
THERESA. Don't do that! I've got a spastic colon!
ANGELICA. Hand me that bottle! *(She does, but hides the book she has removed.)* What are you hiding?
THERESA. The Bible.
ANGELICA. Shame on you — hiding Wild Turkey behind the Bible.

THERESA. I have a sore throat.

ANGELICA. Then gargle. I'll get you some salt.

THERESA. It's not the same. Lend me your hand.

ANGELICA. You got up there by yourself. You can jump down.

THERESA. My teeth will fall out.

ANGELICA. *(Extends a hand.)* I should give you the back of my hand. Sneaking drinks when I'm not here. God will punish you.

THERESA. God is going to punish both of us for pretending to be nuns. Especially since we're good Catholics ... at least on Sunday.

ANGELICA. Well, He hasn't punished us for ten years. I think we're safe. *(Goes to the table and lights a cigarette.)*

THERESA. His eye is on the sparrow, that's why. Deception is a sin.

ANGELICA. If your conscience is bothering you after all these years — go to confession. Then you can sin again with a clear conscience.

THERESA. *(Whimpers.)* I'm running out of churches. Oh, Angelica, I hate being a fraud.

ANGELICA. Well, at least we're respectable frauds.

THERESA. We're sneaky, freaky frauds. We let people put their pennies in our pots thinking it's for a good cause.

ANGELICA. It *is* for a good cause. It's put our darling Tania through college. And it's a much nicer profession than prostitution, according to Reader's Digest.

THERESA. The Bible says, "Woe to him that buildeth his house by unrighteousness."

ANGELICA. It also says, "Woe to the bloody city." We live in what the Bible calls a "generation of vipers."

THERESA. And according to Job 8:13, He warns, "The hypocrite shall perish and his trust shall be a spider web." I hate spiders.

ANGELICA. Well, I know the Bible as well as you do, my dear. As Matthew says, "Ye hypocrite — ye can discern the face of the sky but can ye discern the sign of the times?" Well, you bet I can. It says "survive or sink."

THERESA. Yes, but Luke says, "Thou hypocrite! Doth not each one of you on the Sabbath loose his ass from the stall."

ANGELICA. Well, since neither one of us hustle on Sunday, I think our asses are safe.

THERESA. Matthew says, "Cursed be the deceiver."

ANGELICA. Will you stop hiding behind the Bible. It's bad enough that you use it to hide your Wild Turkey.

THERESA. Well, I can't help worrying. Someday one of us is going to be arrested.

ANGELICA. Theresa dear, stop worrying. You're life expectancy is getting shorter by the minute. Don't waste it worrying. There will be time for that when you get to Heaven.

THERESA. That's what worries me. I may never get there.

ANGELICA. You will if you repent. But wait until you're eighty — that will give you a happy goal to look forward to in your old age.

THERESA. Couldn't we put part of our ill-gotten gains in the poor box at the church? I'd sleep better.

ANGELICA. And have them stolen?

THERESA. Then why couldn't we give a percentage of what we get to the Humane Society or Wayward Girls? Then we'd really be Sisters of Charity. We're already blood sisters.

ANGELICA. We're going to need every cent for Tania's vacation. She wants to go back to Switzerland.

THERESA. I'll go without breakfast .... at least butter.

ANGELICA. Oh, all right. How much do you want to give away to salve your conscience?

THERESA. Twelve percent.

ANGELICA. Why twelve?

THERESA. There were twelve Apostles in the Bible.

ANGELICA. We'll give ten. There are only ten Commandments. What are you doing home this early anyway?

THERESA. I had to go to the toilet.

ANGELICA. You could have gone down to the subway toilet.

THERESA. No! With all those dirty words on the wall. Have you ever seen a nun in a public toilet? Of course not — it's indecent.
ANGELICA. Come to think of it, I've never seen a nun in any toilet — maybe they just dehydrate. Now you better get back to your subway exit, or you'll miss the Bronx traffic going home. *(Sits to count money.)*
THERESA. Angelica, why can't I sit outside of Saks for a change? You meet such a better class of people.
ANGELICA. Because they're rich. And rich people don't give as much as poor people. That's why they're rich.
THERESA. But Bronx people going home from work look so unhappy — as if they have a toothache or hemorrhoids — it depresses me.
ANGELICA. That's because poverty pinches, dear. Have you forgotten?
THERESA. Why do all the working people live in the suburbs? It costs them subway fare to get there and they waste their valuable time getting home to their wives and boiled cabbage.
ANGELICA. Read your Bible. "The poor of the earth hide themselves together." So get back to your post and help them feel noble by taking their money. They probably cheated someone out of it anyhow.
THERESA. *(At the door.)* Couldn't I have just an itsy-bitsy bit of bourbon before I go back just to give me moral strength?
ANGELICA. No! *(Holds up an object.)* What's this? Someone put a Masonic button in your bucket!
THERESA. Maybe it was all some poor soul had.
ANGELICA. Nonsense — people just aren't honest anymore.
THERESA. Isn't that the pot calling the kettle black — begging for a living.
ANGELICA. We do *not* beg. We sit on our little stools and look a little sad. If people want to put their little pennies in our little pots, that's their mistake. Our little pots have put little Tania through college — and art school as well. That's all that matters.
THERESA. I guess you're right. Was there any mail from her

today?

ANGELICA. She's probably too busy painting pictures of saints for French cathedrals.

THERESA. *(Returns from the door.)* Maybe she's sick.

ANGELICA. You can't expect her to write us every day.

THERESA. *We* do. We write *her* every day.

ANGELICA. We'll get a letter tomorrow. *(Hands back the Masonic button.)* And for God sake — will you stop taking buttons! Keep your eyes open! You could be robbed.

THERESA. Maybe she's been run over and God is punishing us.

ANGELICA. God wouldn't punish Tania just to punish us. That's negative thinking. Be optomistic.

THERESA. All right. Maybe she's pregnant.

ANGELICA. Theresa dear, you know damn well that Tania stutters. And girls who stutter rarely get pregnant. But don't ask me why.

THERESA. Why?

ANGELICA. I don't know, dear — maybe that's why she wanted to be an artist. Maybe it's a kind of compensation — to have her paintings speak for her. Lots of famous artists stutter. Michelangelo, Giotto, Da Vinci—

THERESA. Is that true?

ANGELICA. No, but it's a good argument. *(Points to an abstract picture on the wall.)* You like that beautiful painting she sent us, don't you?

THERESA. Oh, I *do* like it, but I wish I knew what it meant.

ANGELICA. It doesn't have to *mean* anything. Does a rose have meaning — a sunset?

THERESA. It means the day is over.

ANGELICA. Well, doesn't her painting make you *Think?*

THERESA. Yes. I think it's upside down.

ANGELICA. Oh, get back to your subway station. I'm trying to add, and I can't add anyway.

THERESA. You're mean to me. And you're bossy, too.

ANGELICA. I am not bossy. I'm efficient. There's a difference.

THERESA. Yes — the difference is they're spelled different.

ANGELICA. *(Puts her arm around Theresa.)* And I'm not mean to you, dear. Whatever I do or say is for your own good.

THERESA. Why is it that everything that's for my own good never feels good, looks good, or tastes good.

ANGELICA. Now you've no grounds for complaint, dear. We're doing all right.

THERESA. We're cheating people. And I hate cheaters.

ANGELICA. Cheating is a respectable, national practice. Ask anyone who pays income tax.

THERESA. I wish I'd married that nice boy, Otis, that was in love with me in high school. His father had the biggest turkey ranch in Pyorrhea, Texas.

ANGELICA. Yes, dear. You could have been Turkey Queen.

THERESA. Do you know for Christmas once, he gave me a life subscription to "Turkey World"? He said if I married him he'd give me a mink coat. Do you think, after we pay for the vacuum cleaner, I could have a mink coat?

ANGELICA. Nuns don't wear mink coats, dear.

THERESA. But I'm not a nun on Sundays. I could wear it to confession.

ANGELICA. A mink coat! I'm ashamed of you. Think of all those poor little minks, and chinchillas, and bunny rabbits that are killed and skinned just to make coats when celanese would do just as well. In my opinion, ladies who lust for mink — stink.

THERESA. Well, you don't get a chill in chincilla, and you can freeze in celanese. As for me, I'd just as soon stink in mink.

ANGELICA. And just where did you read that bit of wisdom?

THERESA. "Turkey World."

ANGELICA. Well, I'll tell you what I'll do, dear. For Christmas I'll buy you a beautiful coat of genuine Russian burlap.

THERESA. We'll probably spend Christmas in jail.

ANGELICA. Nonsense. We've had a successful career, so don't be so glum.

THERESA. I can't help it! I just know one of us is going to be arrested someday — and be hanged. *(Goes to door and stops.)* Well, here I go to the gallows.

ANGELICA. Don't say that! Don't be negative! *(Shouts.)* Be happy!

THERESA. *(Winces.)* All right — I'm happy. *(Grimaces.)* See? And I'll be back in an hour — unless I'm arrested.

ANGELICA. And don't run home. Nuns don't run. I'll have dinner ready. I'll fix eggs Benedict for you. That should cheer you up. St. Benedict was a martyr, too.

THERESA. Eating an egg only depresses me. You're really eating a poor future chicken.

ANGELICA. Well, maybe it will rain. That should make you happy.

THERESA. Well at least it washes the doggy-doo away.

ANGELICA. Oh! Get back to work! You're depressing me. And for Heaven's sake, while you're sitting on your stool, don't whistle either. Nuns don't whistle.

THERESA. Yes, Angelica. *(She exits whistling with her bucket and sign.)*

ANGELICA. *(She sits at table and looks heavenward.)* Oh Lord, look after my dear, dumb sister. She means well. But, you know what happens to well-meaning people — they always get run over by a dump truck or ambulance. *(She begins to count coins again, singing, "I Got The Whole World In My Hands." After a moment, she rises.)* Well, that's that ... as the mortician said when he closed the coffin. *(Starts out, sighing.)* Oh, my aching back. I wish I were born eighty years old and grew younger as I got older. I could end my days happily back in my dear mother's womb instead of a wheelchair or the grave. Of course, by the time I got back to the womb, Mother would be a hundred and ten. Oh, well. *(She goes into the kitchen. After a few moments, a knotted rope descends from the skylight. A handsome young man in a jumpsuit descends the rope. He looks around stealthily and quickly steps out of his jumpsuit. He is now clothed in only trunks, tennis shoes, and a card on his back on which the number "13" is printed. He sees the money on the table and scoops it into a small bag he carries. Just as he finishes, the telephone rings. He darts behind a sofa. Angelica enters with an apron around her waist and carrying a large butcher knife. Into phone.)* Hello. What? *Who* did you want? The rabbi? I'm sorry, but you have the wrong number. This is the city morgue. *(She hangs up.)* Why is it that there are more horses' asses than there are horses? *(She stops suddenly on her way back to the kitchen. It now registers that she has seen a rope hanging from the skylight. She returns and studies it.)* Now, I'm sure that wasn't here before. *(Looks up.)* Anybody up there? Jack and the Beanstalk? The Lord? The landlord? *(She sees that her money is gone.)* Hoho! Mice! *(She brandishes her knife as she looks behind the sofa and sees the thief.)* Lose something, young man? *(The boy rises. Angelica gasps as she sees him.)* Billy! No — no!

BOY. Oh, my God — you're a nun!

ANGELICA. For a moment I thought — but you couldn't be. Billy wasn't a thief. And he's dead. *(Points to the table.)* What happened to my money?

BOY. I'll give it back. I don't steal from nuns. Honest. I got principles. You think I want God to strike me dead? In shorts?

ANGELICA. He won't have to — *I* will! Now, you put that money right back before I call the police.

BOY. *(Puts money back.)* I'm sorry, Sister. I didn't know there were nuns here. Believe me! They told me only prostitutes lived in this building. That's why I picked it out. I'm sort of doing God's work.

ANGELICA. Well, now I've heard everything. You ought to be ashamed of yourself — a healthy, handsome kid like you, climbing down a rope like a monkey to steal money from prostitutes — money they've honestly earned.

BOY. You don't understand. I only steal for a good cause.

ANGELICA. *What* good cause?

BOY. I'm a medical student. I'm educating myself.

ANGELICA. You're a *what?*

BOY. I'm studying to be a doctor. This is the only way I can raise my tuition. Do you know what it is going to cost me to get my doctor's degree?

ANGELICA. Yes. And I can tell you in one word. It's going to cost you your integrity. *(She then adds.)* Your honesty, self-respect, ethics, nobility, scruples, duty, objectivity, patriotism, moral standards, probity, candor, veracity, and honor. All those lofty hazards that hinder survival.

BOY. I'm going to need at least eighty thousand dollars in tuition fees before I can hang out my shingle.

ANGELICA. Eighty thousand! Why, that's highway robbery!

BOY. I know. That's what gave me this idea.

ANGELICA. So you're forced to steal to study?

BOY. I don't call it stealing. I'm keeping a list and I'm going to pay every cent back with interest when I'm a famous doctor. I'm honest.

ANGELICA. What if people find out you've been stealing after you're famous? Won't that cost you patients?

BOY. When a famous doctor becomes a famous doctor, who cares how he became a famous doctor, if he's that famous? No one cares how you've got money as long as you've got it.

ANGELICA. You know, you're as nimble at excuses as you are on a rope — you just might hang yourself.

BOY. Please don't turn me in, Sister. Be a Christian nun. Save *me* and think of all the lives you'll save in the future because you saved me now.

ANGELICA. What kind of doctor are you going to be? A brain doctor?

BOY. An obstetrician.

ANGELICA. An obstetrician for Heaven's sake!

BOY. No. For my mother's sake. I was told that she died at sixteen giving birth to me, and I want to repay her for giving up her life for mine.

ANGELICA. You're either the greatest liar I've ever met or the most naive. Why are you wearing that indecent outfit?

BOY. If a cop sees me running, he'll just think I'm jogging. Sometimes they even wave back at me.

ANGELICA. You know, I think you *will* be famous.

BOY. Are you going to turn me in?

ANGELICA. No. I'm going to help you — fool that I am.

BOY. Oh, thank you, Sister. You're a saint. *(Kisses her hand.)*

ANGELICA. Sit down — you're getting me all wet. How old are you?
BOY. Nineteen. *(Adds.)* Going on twenty.
ANGELICA. That sounds like you're timing an egg. But then, I'm forty-eight going on thirty-nine. Who are your parents?
BOY. God knows.
ANGELICA. Well, that's a valid assumption. But don't you have any inside information?
BOY. *(Shrugs.)* I was an orphan. I was raised in an orphanage until I was kicked out at fifteen.
ANGELICA. No one adopted you?
BOY. No one wanted me. I was too fat.
ANGELICA. Well, you've lost your baby fat and someone's lost a handsome son.
BOY. It's nice of you to say that.
ANGELICA. That's why I said it. How did you happen to get into medical school instead of jail?
BOY. Luck. I had a job as an orderly in a hospital. A wonderful old doctor there took a liking to me and helped me get through college. I majored in philosophy.
ANGELICA. It shows. Where is your benefactor now?
BOY. Heaven, I guess. If he isn't, I don't want to go there.
ANGELICA. Haven't I seen your life story on television?
BOY. Every week.
ANGELICA. Well, you've plenty of time to work your way into Heaven — so don't rush it. How much money do you need at the moment?
BOY. Why?
ANGELICA. That's a stupid answer to a leading question. *(Points to the table.)* Count your blessings and count out what you need. Buy some medical books on senility. I may need your help soon.
BOY. Oh, I couldn't take money from a nun. I'm dedicated, too.
ANGELICA. Take it. I'm buying my way into Heaven.
BOY. No. I'd feel corrupted. What order do you belong to,

Sister?
ANGELICA. Sisters of Charity. Take it.
BOY. No.
ANGELICA. Take it or I'll call a cop.
BOY. No, I'm an idealist.
ANGELICA. You're an idiot. Let me give you some advice my piss-poor old mother — God rest her soul — once gave me. She said, "Money talks. Sometimes it sings. If you don't have it, you sing for your supper. Rich people sleep on satin sheets — poor people sleep on empty stomachs. Rich people wipe their mouths — poor people lick their fingers. Rich people have Cadillacs to drive them home — poor people have kids to drive them crazy. Rich people have golf — poor people have God. Rich people go to psychiatrists — poor people go to confession. Rich people pay for their luxuries — poor people pay for their sins." So stuff that in your pipe, son, and smoke it! *(Whacks him on the shoulder.)* And take whatever you need there— *(Points to money.)* —and stuff that in your *pocket.*
BOY. Well, I wouldn't want to offend you by refusing your blessing. *(Takes money.)* Why are you doing this for me?
ANGELICA. I was dropped on my head as a baby.
BOY. I'm going to mention you in my prayers every night, Sister.
ANGELICA. I wouldn't if I were you. Are you hungry?
BOY. Just for knowledge.
ANGELICA. Well, that's something you can digest but it doesn't put on weight. Come in the kitchen and I'll give you some food for thought. *(Starts for kitchen.)*
BOY. *(Follows.)* You know, Sister, I've never met a nun like you before.
ANGELICA. You're luckier than you know.
BOY. *(Points to skylight.)* Shall I take my rope down?
ANGELICA. No. Wait til my sister comes back. I want to remind her that life is full of knots. *(They go out. After a few moments the front door opens and Theresa enters followed by a fat cop carrying her collection bucket and stool.)*

COP. This is where you live?
THERESA. Yes, sir.
COP. This ain't no convent.
THERESA. No, sir. We're retired.
COP. Where's this sister you mentioned?
THERESA. Fixing dinner. I'll call her, sir. *(Calls.)* Angelica! Angelica, dear— I'm home. Angelica! *(To cop.)* That's her name, sir — Angelica. That's why I call her Angelica. *(Smiles beguilingly.)*
COP. *(Points to rope.)* What's that rope for?
THERESA. I guess our laundry line fell down. This whole building is falling down. I fell down the steps yesterday and spilled the garbage in a baby carriage... made the mother mad... she called me something in Spanish. *(Angelica enters and stops on seeing an officer.)*
ANGELICA. Who's he?
THERESA. He's a cop.
ANGELICA. What'd you bring him *here* for?
THERESA. He brought me. *(She starts to sob. The cop hands Theresa his handkerchief.)*
COP. Here, take this... I ain't used it yet. *(Turns to Angelica.)* Are you this Sister's sister, Sister?
ANGELICA. No— I'm her *mother*. Her Mother Superior. What business is that of yours?
COP. Police business. I'm charging her with begging without a license. *(Theresa wails.)*
ANGELICA. What is she — a dog? She has to have a license?
COP. You're close. In this here city, you want a car, a wife, or a dog, you gotta get a license.
ANGELICA. *(To Theresa.)* Were you doing anything to attract a cop's attention?
THERESA. Nothing, Angelica. Honest. I was just sitting on my little stool eating an ice cream cone.
ANGELICA. Officer, begging is an honorable profession. Don't you read the Bible? The Lord loved the beggars.
COP. Well, Mayor Horowitz don't. I read the Police Manual and

that book says it's thirty days for begging without a license. In this here civilized city you gotta pay to be a public nuisance.

ANGELICA. But the Bible tells you what your duty is too, Officer. It says, "He raiseth up the poor out of the dust and lifteth up the beggar from the dunghill." Samuel, Chapter 2.

THERESA. Dunghill?

COP. Well, the New Official Revised Ordinance Code and Municipal Corrective Police Authority Amended Manual says you gotta pay to beg here. Horowitz, Chapter 10.

ANGELICA. But, sir, which will get you into Heaven, the Bible or the New Official Revised Ordinance Code and Municipal Corrective Police Authority Amended Manual?

COP. Well, the New Official Revised Ordinance Code and Municipal Corrective Police Authority Amended Manual is *my* Bible. And that says to put her into the pokey pronto.

ANGELICA. Have you forgotten that Lazarus was a blind beggar and the good Lord gave him back his eyesight. The least you can do is give her back her pot.

COP. I'll give her a free ride to the clink. *(To Theresa.)* Are you ready, Sister? *(Theresa wails.)*

ANGELICA. Oh, stop keening. No one's dead. Yet. *(To cop.)* Why don't you mug a mugger instead of pinching a nun? Don't you have a mother?

COP. Well, I wasn't incubated.

ANGELICA. What's she going to say when you go home tonight and tell her that you arrested a Sister of Charity?

COP. She ain't home.

ANGELICA. Well, wherever she is.

COP. She's been dead twenty years, so I stopped telling her what I do. *(To Theresa.)* Come on. I'm double-parked and I don't want to get a ticket.

ANGELICA. In a police car?

COP. It's a stolen Toyota we picked up. *(He takes Theresa's elbow and she wails again.)*

ANGELICA. Will you stop that! You're not a coyote. *(Then sweetly to the cop.)* Now, Officer, you look like a good man.

COP. I do?
ANGELICA. Well, I haven't got my glasses. But, I'm sure you're a good father.
COP. I hope not. I'm not married.
ANGELICA. How did that happen — a handsome beast like you?
COP. *(Shrugs.)* When I was young, I was too friggin' poor. And, when I got older, I was too friggin' smart.
ANGELICA. Oh, a true philosopher. Well, anyhow, why don't you be a good Boy Scout and just forget this. You'll feel noble and exalted. Pity and forgiveness can be intoxicating. You like to drink, don't you?
THERESA. I do.
COP. I don't drink on duty. I got ideals and an ulcer.
ANGELICA. But this is a rare opportunity for you to become a saint. Have you ever heard of a cop being canonized? No! This is your chance for Heavenly promotion.
COP. *(Ponders.)* Well, taking her down to the station would take up an hour of my time.
ANGELICA. And time is money.
COP. And waste another hour of the judge's time to sentence her. *(Theresa wails.)*
ANGELICA. Waste not — want not.
COP. And cost the city money to feed her for thirty days. *(Theresa wails again.)*
ANGELICA. A penny saved is a penny earned.
COP. So I'll tell you what ... I'll let her go this time.
THERESA. You will! He will! *(She grabs his hand and kisses it madly.)* You're an angel!
ANGELICA. You're a saint!
COP. For fifty dollars. *(Theresa wails.)*
ANGELICA. You want to be paid to let her go!
THERESA. Call a cop, Angelica, have him arrested.
COP. I'll call one for you. We'll split the fifty, fifty-fifty.
THERESA. *(Waves a finger under his nose.)* You're a thief! A crooked crook!

COP. I'm a good citizen. I'm saving the city time and money.
ANGELICA. You don't need a gun. Extortion is a far better weapon for a crook. Your victims only bleed financially.
COP. Lemme tell you somethin', Sister. In this here model city if you wanna run a bar, a hotel, a boat, a garage, or a bus, you gotta have a license. You wanna be a pilot, a promoter, or a pushpeddler you gotta get a permit. You wanna sell booze, bagels, bug-bombs, butter, or bicycles, you need a license. Down at City Hall they gotta list of eight hundred ways to tax you. It's their gimmick for gettin' a kickback. And it's from them bums I learned my way to get mine. So, just gimme fifty bucks and my handkerchief and I'll get the hell out of here. I won't say nothin'. You can trust me. By comparison, I'm a downright honest cop.
ANGELICA. I'm glad to hear that because that means you're down and out with no honest right to be dishonest.
COP. Well, I'm honest about being crooked, then.
ANGELICA. I'm glad to hear that, too. Honesty should always have a positive purpose. Otherwise, it's like kissing yourself in a mirror. Shall I get you a mirror?
COP. *(Studies her.)* How'd you get so smart?
ANGELICA. I went to night school.
COP. *(Points to Theresa.)* How'd she get so dumb?
THERESA. I went to sleep.
COP. Well, my deal is fifty bucks. Take it or leave it. *(Theresa wails.)*
ANGELICA. Oh, stop baying at the moon. *(To cop.)* All right, you poor motherless bastard — we'll pay. *(Hands him money.)* There are prostitutes, junkies, and bookies in this building. Why don't you collect from them?
COP. What makes you think I don't?
THERESA. He's not honest, Angelica.
COP. Well, I don't steal or beg.
ANGELICA. No? Do you report this supplemental income when you file your tax return?
COP. No — do you?
ANGELICA. With your sense of public dedication, you should

run for a public office.
COP. It's too easy to get caught.
ANGELICA. Could I ask a question for my fifty dollars? Just a hypothetical question.
COP. Hypothetical question? Don't that mean you got somethin' to hide?
ANGELICA. What would happen if someone pretended to be someone and somehow someone caught them somehow?
COP. You mean like you and her pretending to be nuns?
ANGELICA. *(Innocently.)* What*ever* can you mean?
COP. Oh, I've known all along that you two weren't really nuns.
ANGELICA and THERESA. *(Together.)* You did!
COP. I wouldn't take no money from no *real* nuns. You must think I'm a shit.
ANGELICA. You said it — I didn't.
THERESA. Maybe he isn't a real cop, Angelica.
ANGELICA. Are you?
COP. Honest to God.
ANGELICA. Got any identification?
COP. Yes — a badge and a strawberry birthmark on my ass. Which one do you want to see?
ANGELICA. You know, Officer, with your distorted sense of values maybe we ought to be in business together. Maybe Heaven has sent you after all. I've got an idea. *(To Theresa.)* Theresa, dear — there's a young man in the kitchen eating a pastrami sandwich. Get him for me, please. You can't miss him — he's half naked.
THERESA. *(Goes to kitchen door.)* Well, that's a surprise. I didn't know we had any pastrami. *(She goes out. The cop looks at the rope.)*
COP. What's the rope for?
ANGELICA. It's a shortcut to the roof. I like to feed the pigeons.
COP. I never seen no nun climbing no rope.
ANGELICA. There are many ways to get to Heaven.
COP. How long have you two dames been getting away with this

hocus-pocus-holy-hustling?
ANGELICA. When was Lincoln shot?
COP. Lincoln who?
ANGELICA. You know — I like you. There's something very refreshing about you — like a good bathroom deodorant.
COP. I like you too, Sister. You come up with a good racket. I admire that in a woman. *(Theresa returns with the boy.)*
ANGELICA. This young man is a dear, dear friend of mine. What's your name, son?
BOY. Benjamin. In Hebrew that means "son of my right hand."
ANGELICA. Very apt — it doesn't know what your left is doing.
COP. You Jewish?
BEN. Why? Are you prejudiced?
COP. Me? I don't take no chances no more. Last year I met a nice black guy at a bar. We got along fine till I told him I'd once shot a coon. He slugged me. I meant a *rac*coon. I'm no bigot. I love niggers.
ANGELICA. Please! *(Points to Theresa.)* Now this is Sister Theresa, my sister, and your name is— *(Turns to the cop.)*
COP. Bozo. My mother hated my father, and she named me after the dog to spite him. When she would call me, we both came running. The dog got better treatment than me.
ANGELICA. Do you have a last name? Dogs usually don't.
BOZO. Fettuccine.
ANGELICA. That's a pasta — that's not a name — even for a dog.
BOZO. To a Sicilian, it's mother's milk — and it's better than Fink.
ANGELICA. Not much. *(To Ben.)* And Benjamin, this is my sister, Theresa. She feeds ants and talks to flowers.
BEN. Doesn't everyone?
THERESA. Oh, I *like* you! You're witty.
BEN. Only by contrast to an aardvark.
THERESA. Isn't he funny, Angelica?

ANGELICA. Hilarious. *(Turns to Ben.)* Benjamin, I have something to tell you about my sister and myself that may disillusion you. We are not really nuns.
BEN. What are you? Actors in a play?
ANGELICA. You could put it that way. Our word "hypocrite" comes from the Greek word "hypokrites" meaning actor ... so I guess the shoe fits. We dress up as nuns and sit at subway exits with our little pots, and look sad.
THERESA. And people put money in our little pots. We don't even have to ask.
BEN. That's a great idea! Do you suppose I could dress up as a nun, too?
THERESA. At least you'd be a pretty nun.
ANGELICA. Now, you may well ask why we do this.
BEN. All right, I'll ask. Why do you?
ANGELICA. I'm glad you asked. It's a sad story, so get out your handkerchiefs while Theresa plays her sobbing violin.
THERESA. I don't have a violin.
ANGELICA. We had a younger brother we adored. He was killed in a car accident with his darling young wife, leaving us with a baby girl to raise.
BOZO. Didn't I see that in a movie?
ANGELICA. Probably. It happens in life. And because the accident was poor Billy's fault, we were sued for every cent we had. Neither one of us was qualified for any kind of job. I couldn't type, and God knows I couldn't spell.
THERESA. I tried to be a waitress in a terrible nightclub called the Armpit. I had to wear a bunny tail. Sailors pinched my behind. I wasn't happy.
ANGELICA. I was forced to take a night job cleaning floors in an office building. One rainy night on my way home I stopped under an awning. When I put my hand out to see if it had stopped raining, a passing drunk in a tuxedo put a dollar bill in it.
BEN. He thought you were begging?
ANGELICA. Well, I must have looked like Dracula's sister. Anyhow, it dawned on me then, if people would give you money

without you even asking, we'd found the answer to our problem. Thus we became sad and silent Sisters of Charity.
BEN. You sure fooled me.
BOZO. Not me. I knew they was phonies when I seen her... *(Points to Theresa.)* ...in a bar with her nose in a glass of suds.
ANGELICA. Theresa! You went into a saloon?
THERESA. I had to go to the toilet.
BEN. What happened to the kid your brother left you?
ANGELICA. We sent her to Switzerland to be educated. She grew up never knowing where the money came from. She is in Paris now at art school. Someday she'll be famous. *(Points.)* That's one of her paintings there on the wall.
BOZO. Who's it suppose to be?
ANGELICA. It's not a who. It's an abstract ... that means you don't have to understand it.
BOZO. I like pictures of the ocean.
ANGELICA. I'll get you a steamship calendar or some salt water.
BOZO. Well, you done what you done for a good cause, so I'm gonna give you back twenty-five of the fifty you give me.
ANGELICA. No. I want you to keep it as a reward, because you've given me an idea of how we can all make a lot of money if we all work together.
BOZO. Well, I ain't gonna dress up like no nun.
ANGELICA. Heaven forbid! *(Turns to Theresa.)* Theresa, dear, get us some coffee and donuts. I want to have a long conference with Captain Bozo here about our future.
THERESA. *(Cups her hands and shouts toward kitchen.)* Four javas coming up! *(Turns to them and beams.)* I learned that in that awful restaurant I worked in — The Upper Montclair Armpit. *(She lifts her dress and races into the kitchen. Ben sits at the table between Bozo and Angelica. As he listens to their conversation, his head swivels back and forth as if watching a tennis game.)*
BOZO. She's got good gams.
ANGELICA. Let's stick to business. Now if we're to form a partnership, I think you owe me some sort of character reference.

So, may I ask you why you started collecting kickbacks? I know one of the fringe benefits of fraud is its consoling sense of justification. What's yours?
BOZO. Like you, I got my reasons, too.
ANGELICA. May I ask what your good cause is?
BOZO. My mother's tombstone. Ten years now, and she ain't got no marker on her last resting place. She's laying out there alone like she was living on a street with no zip code.
ANGELICA. Is she expecting someone to write her?
BOZO. No, but it ain't respectable not to have no marble stone on top of you to let people know where you're at.
ANGELICA. Particularly when you settle down in one place permanently.
BOZO. So I'm saving up to get her a stone statue of a big-as-life marble angel with big, long wings hanging down below her ass that will make all them other tombstones look like shithouses.
ANGELICA. Officer, did anyone ever tell you that you have a touch of the poet?
BOZO. I got my moments.
ANGELICA. You must enrich us more often. You're obviously a man of great culture. May I ask where you were educated?
BOZO. Dart-mouth *(His accent is on the word "mouth.")*
ANGELICA. Dartmouth? Was your father a professor?
BOZO. Janitor. I got me my education watching them rich kids getting *their* education.
ANGELICA. How astute — if you'll pardon the expression.
BOZO. But I hadda get out and hustle before I was sixteen.
ANGELICA. Did your father lose his job?
BOZO. You could say that. He was electrocuted.
ANGELICA. He committed a crime?
BOZO. Well, he done something foolish.
ANGELICA. It's always foolish to get caught. What did he do?
BOZO. He took a bath. He put his radio on the edge of the tub and it fell into the water and electrocuted him. And he was listenin' to Billy Graham, too. That's a helluva way to die, ain't it?

ANGELICA. There are very few good ways left.

BOZO. But I ain't done bad for myself. I got two color TV sets and a stolen Toyota.

ANGELICA. So you learned duplicity and avarice at the school of life.

BOZO. What's avarice?

ANGELICA. It's a kind of yogurt that restores financial deficiencies.

BOZO. How'd you get so smart?

ANGELICA. I went to night school while other people went to sleep.

BOZO. Yeah. That's the trouble with the whole damn human race. They go to sleep and let mice and rats eat their cheese.

ANGELICA. You know, Officer Bozo, you have a rather unique mentality. It seeks the essential truth with unerring instinct. It's sort of like a sky-born buzzard that can see a rabbit in the grass far below him. To watch your mind zero in on the core of credibility is like watching a helicopter landing in a paddy fireld. I hope you take that as a compliment.

BOZO. Sister, I learned a long time ago when you don't understand something, take it as a compliment. *(Turns to Ben.)* Well, ain't you got nothin' to say?

BEN. Say what?

BOZO. Whatever you been thinkin'.

BEN. I was thinking that I would write a novel. *(At this point, Theresa returns with a tray.)*

ANGELICA. What took you so long, dear?

THERESA. I was picking ants out of the sugar.

ANGELICA. Well, thanks to the ants I had a chance to become acquainted with Officer Bozo. Sit down, dear, and I'll tell you what my plan is. *(To Bozo.)* You need money for your mother's tombstone. We need money to keep our darling Tania in Paris. *(To Ben.)* Ben here needs money to finish medical school ... he's going to be a doctor.

BOZO. A dentist? I could use one.

ANGELICA. An obstetrician. And that will take him eight or nine

years.
BOZO. What's an obstetrician?
ANGELICA. That's a specialist who takes care of expectant mothers.
BOZO. Great! I'll come to him when I get pregnant. That'll take me eight or nine years.
ANGELICA. Now if we join forces, we can all benefit. *(To Bozo.)* You can give us protection and we'll drum up new business for you.
BOZO. What kind of business?
ANGELICA. I'm coming to that. We know of a lot of building violations in this one block alone. We can make up a list for you to get kickbacks, and we'd be doing it for a good cause. We'll be improving the neighborhood or at least your financial standing.
BOZO. It sounds like dirty pool — I like it.
ANGELICA. And in return for the information we furnish you, you can kick back twenty percent of whatever kickback *you* collect.
BOZO. Make it ten.
ANGELICA. Fifteen.
BOZO. Thirteen.
THERESA. Thirteen is unlucky. Take twelve, Angelica. Remember the Apostles.
BOZO. All right, twelve percent then. I been raped.
ANGELICA. Now, there's a restaurant on the corner that's a disgrace to public health. Every time I go in there I see a rat in the kitchen.
BOZO. The cook or the owner?
ANGELICA. A real rat on the food counter.
BOZO. That's terrible. Some places got no pride.
BEN. Where do I come in?
ANGELICA. We'll make you a legitimate businessman above reproach.
BEN. That'll take money, won't it?
ANGELICA. Not really. We'll get you some dark glasses, a tin cup, a white cane and a Seeing Eye dog. Bozo can pick out a nice

area where you can operate safely.

BOZO. I'd rent you my dog, only it's blind.

ANGELICA. We'll go to the pound and pick out a sad-looking dog for you — a beagle, if we can. They look sad even when they're happy.

BOZO. Hey, I got a great idea to give Ben class. I got a buddy on the force that's got a three-legged dog. Maybe I could steal it.

BEN. No. I've got to live with my dog, and I want to get one I can love.

BOZO. You're too soft, kid. With a three-legged dog, you'd break every hustler's heart on Broadway.

THERESA. Could I have a cat, Angelica? I once had a girlfriend named Kitty. She lived on Pussy Willow Street. Don't you think that's interesting?

ANGELICA. Not particularly. Anyhow, we won't have room. Ben will move in here with us and keep the dog in the bathroom.

THERESA. I don't think they allow dogs in this building. Only prostitutes.

BOZO. I can fix that.

ANGELICA. Now, if we're going to form an organization, we should all take an oath to be completely honest with each other. No sticky fingers.

THERESA. If we're an organization, shouldn't we have some kind of nice slogan? Something like "Help the Handicapped?"

ANGELICA. We're not handicapped, dear.

THERESA. We are too, we're incompetent.

ANGELICA. Theresa dear, get mother's old Bible. It's next to the Boston Cookbook.

THERESA. *(To Ben.)* Ben, why don't you name your dog after one in the Bible? Don't you think that would be nice?

ANGELICA. Theresa, there's no dog mentioned in the Bible.

THERESA. There is too ... it was called "Moreover." It says in the Bible that Naboth lay dying on the ground and moreover the dog came up and licked his wounds.

BEN. I think I'll name my dog Hippocrates.

BOZO. Is that your father's name?
BEN. No, Hippocrates was the father of medicine.
BOZO. Yeah ... Hippie is a good name for a dog.
THERESA. *(Returns with Bible and hands it to Angelica.)* Be careful if you open it. I've got some violets pressed in Proverbs.
ANGELICA. Now, everyone place your right hand on the Bible. *(They do.)* Now repeat after me. "Dear God—
ALL. Dear God.
ANGELICA. "Who loves the poor and needy—
ALL. Who loves the poor and needy.
ANGELICA. "May you strike us dead—
BOZO. This is an oath!
ANGELICA. An oath of trust and loyalty. Say it.
ALL. May you strike us dead.
THERESA. I hope God's eye is on the sparrow.
ANGELICA. "If we ever betray each other—
ALL. If we ever betray each other.
ANGELICA. "Amen."
ALL. Amen.
ANGELICA. Now, having taken our oath of allegiance, we can consider ourselves a conglomerate, dedicated to those high ideals of industry .... to the A.B.C.'s of big business, "Avarice" ... "Bullshit" ... and "Cupidity."
BEN. Hear! Hear!
ANGELICA. *(Looking heavenward.)* And, dear Lord ... please remember ... You love sinners. And sinners make the best saints.
ALL. *(Loudly.)* A ... men!! *(Theresa starts singing "Onward Christian Soldiers.")*

CURTAIN

ACT II

PLACE — The same.

TIME — Several weeks later.

AT RISE — As in the first act, no one is on stage at curtain rise. After a moment, the hall door opens and a small woebegone mongrel appears on a leash. The dog is followed by Benjamin, wearing dark glasses and carrying a white cane and tin cup.

BEN. You were a good doggie today, Hippie — you didn't lead me into a single manhole ... or nosey cop. *(He hooks the leash over a chair and goes to the large bowl on the table. He empties the contents of his cup and pockets into the bowl.)* That sad look of yours, old boy, is money in the bank. *(The dog ignores him. He squats in front of the pooch.)* How would you like a nice big bowl of gourmet horse meat? *(Straightens.)* I'll get it for you — don't get up. You know, you almost got me killed today, leading me in front of that garbage truck just to sniff that poodle you saw. Instead of giving you horse meat, I really should give you a kick in the ass. But that's all right because you're my buddy and you wouldn't remember anyhow. You're handsome but you've got the memory span of a gnat. *(He pats the dog and goes into kitchen. He returns after a moment and places a dog bowl on the floor which the dog ignores. [Note: Gasoline or something objectionable should be used to deter the dog's interest in the bowl.] After a moment of waiting.)* Well, there it is, stupid. Can't you see it? You're supposed to be a Seeing Eye dog. *(He waits and then pretends to stick his finger in the dog's food. He then licks his finger.)* Mmmmm! *Good!* Come on, just taste it ... it's full of nice goodies all dogs just love ... it has some tasty fiber in it and nice crude fat and bone meal and salubrious soybean, dried fish and exciting brewer's yeast.

29

(Yells.) Eat it! You eat everything else we pass in the street. This comes out of a can instead of a horse. *(Gets down on his knees and prays to dog.) Please* eat it. For me. For your own sake ... for God's sake! Your hair is falling out. Eat a little. You're making me sound like a Jewish mother. Eat a little. *(Waits and picks dog up.)* All right, then ... come on, I'll give you a bath. I don't mind sleeping with you but you smell bad. *(Starts out.)* Of course, maybe human beings smell bad to you. If it'll make you happy, I'll get in the tub with you. *(They go out. After a moment, the hall door opens and Bozo enters. He is dressed in his usual cop uniform. He also carries a briefcase. He hangs up top coat.)*

BOZO. Anybody home in the do-ma-sill?

BEN. *(Answers from offstage.)* I'm in the bathroom.

BOZO. What are you doing in the bathroom?

BEN. What do you think — I'm giving the dog a bath.

BOZO. Wanna give *me* a bath?

BEN. There's not enough soap.

BOZO. Smart ass. *(He goes to the kitty and empties money from his briefcase into the bowl. He looks furtively around and takes out one bill. He hides it in the pocket of his topcoat, which is hanging on a hook.)*

BEN. *(Offstage.)* Help! Bozo ... help me!

BOZO. What's a matter? *(Ben, a towel around his waist, staggers onstage, hands outstretched.)*

BEN. I've got soap in my eyes. I can't see!

BOZO. Well, we can't afford no blind blindman. *(Pushes him down into a chair.)* Here, I'll get it out for you. *(He takes out his handkerchief and wipes Ben's eyes.)* How the hell did you get soap in your *eyes?*

BEN. My dog tried to kiss me.

BOZO. A dame did that to me once. By the time I got the suds out of my eyes, she'd stolen my wallet and gone. I'd have chased her, only she'd stolen my pants, too. *(He spits on his handkerchief and wipes Ben's eyes again.)*

BEN. All Hippie wants is my love and attention, and a dog biscuit. And he's got all those. I've learned to love that dog.

BOZO. *(Sniffs Ben.)* You got some new kind of cologne on?

BEN. It's something new called "Deception." I thought it was the proper smell for someone pretending to be blind.

BOZO. It stinks.

BEN. Well, so does what I'm doing. *(He walks away.)* Thanks.

BOZO. I don't see nobody standin' behind you with a gun, buddy.

BEN. *(Goes to mirror to look at his eyes.)* Of course not. You can't see them. But they're all out there with their guns in your back saying, "Get out of my way."

BOZO. Then get smart — get yours — get out or get lost. *(He takes a banana from the fruitbowl by the window and peels it.)*

BEN. I'm learning. So I dab a little "Deception" on, and at least I smell better. *(Bozo looks around, and then throws the banana peel out of the window.)*

BOZO. You know, I've been thinkin'. It might be a good idea, since we're all working together, if I moved in here with the three of you.

BEN. Where would you sleep?

BOZO. Well, you gotta big bed. *(Points to bedroom.)*

BEN. Yeah, you've gotta big ass.

BOZO. Think of the overhead we'd be savin'. One telephone bill — one light bill — one stove — one refrigerator — one rent for one big happy family.

BEN. With one bathroom. *(He starts out.)*

BOZO. And one car. On Sunday we could all go to church together in my stolen Toyota.

BEN. Sounds inspired. People who steal together should kneel together.

BOZO. I think it's a helluva idea. A closed corporation.

BEN. Look, Bozo ... I sleep with my dog. I don't think you'd be happy in bed with me.

BOZO. Why? Do you snore?

BEN. No, but my dog passes wind in his sleep.

BOZO. Well, if you don't mind him, you won't mind me. I do the same. *(He follows Ben out. After a moment, Angelica enters in her nun's habit.)*

ANGELICA. Anyone here besides the mice?

BOZO. *(Offstage.)* Just us dogs.

ANGELICA. Where are you?

BOZO. I'm in the bathtub with Ben.

ANGELICA. Together?

BOZO. We're washin' the dog.

ANGELICA. Well, wash the tub out when you're through. I want to take a bath myself. *(She goes to the bowl and empties contents of her little red pot into the kitty. She then removes her nun's headdress or wimple.)* That dirty crook of a landlord stopped me on the stairs again. Those prostitutes on the ground floor complained about having a couple of nuns in this building. They said it gave them a bad reputation. *(Ben enters carrying his wet, dripping dog in a towel. He is followed by Bozo also with a towel. Ben puts the docile dog on the floor and kneels to finish drying him.)*

BEN. I hope you told him off.

ANGELICA. I did. Politely, of course. I simply said, "Sir, I wish you many, many years of hardship and misery, with dozens of mongoloid children all looking like gremlins and if I can ever be of disservice, don't hesitate to call on me. And I trust you won't take this personally."

BOZO. He's lucky you didn't lose your temper.

ANGELICA. I never lose my temper, Bozo.... just my keys, my sense of humor, and my faith in man's inherent decency.

BOZO. Want me to kick him in the ass for you?

ANGELICA. No thanks. The poor man suffers from a terminal affliction.

BEN. He does?

BOZO. What?

ANGELICA. His wife.

BOZO. I know. I seen her. I'm sorry to say, I feel sorry for the poor bastard.

ANGELICA. Never feel sorry for an enemy, Bozo. They couldn't care less. Just be sorry you have one.

BEN. *(Picks up dog.)* Come on, pal. I'll spray you with some nice cologne. *(He carries dog out.)*

BOZO. *(Points to table.)* I already put my take in the kitty. I don't even have bus fare left. *(He follows Ben out. Angelica stands thoughtfully for a moment and then goes to Bozo's topcoat and goes through his pockets. She finds the stolen bill.)*

ANGELICA. Bus fare? Twenty dollars? Is there no honesty left in this dishonest world? *(She takes the bill back to the table and adds it to the kitty. She calls toward the bathroom.)* Hold the dog in there, Ben. I finally got his dog license. *(Starts toward bathroom.)* At least we'll make him legitimate. *(She goes into the hallway. Theresa enters carrying her stool and little red pot. She seems to limp a little.)*

THERESA. Angelica? It's me. Where are *you?*

ANGELICA. *(Offstage.)* I'm in the bathroom with Ben and Bozo.

THERESA. What are all three of you doing in the bathroom?

ANGELICA. Cooking your eggs Benedict ... what did you think?

THERESA. Well, I just wondered. I hope you don't take too long. I have to go to the toilet. I had a bad fall downstairs. I slipped on a banana peel. *(She empties her "take" into the kitty, then, beaming happily, she takes a bottle of bourbon from the folds of her costume and hastens to a flower stand. She empties the liquor into a watering can. She looks around for some place to dispose of the empty bottle. She decides against throwing it out the window, and hides it instead in one of Bozo's topcoat pockets. She then returns to the flower stand and takes a long swig from the spout of the watering can. She hides the can behind a fern and goes happily limping back to the table.)*

ANGELICA. What are you smirking about? You look like the cat that swallowed the canary. *(Kisses Theresa and gives her a hug.)*

THERESA. That's because I had a wonderful day. A nice priest put a twenty dollar bill in my little pot. *(Shows the bill.)*

ANGELICA. Did he ask you any questions?

THERESA. Just my name.

ANGELICA. What did you say?

THERESA. No speak English.

ANGELICA. That was very clever of you, dear, but you really don't look Puerto Rican.

THERESA. He gave me his blessing, too. I kissed his hand.
ANGELICA. Well, that was going far enough. *(Examines bill.)* And this is the bill he gave you?
THERESA. Could we keep it and frame it? After all, it's kind of sacred.
ANGELICA. Why not? It's counterfeit.
THERESA. A counterfeit! Do you think he knew?
ANGELICA. He probably wasn't even a real priest.
THERESA. You mean he was making money to make money?
ANGELICA. Be glad you only kissed his hand.
THERESA. But he looked so honest.
ANGELICA. Never go by looks, dear ... poison oak looks like ivy and poison ivy looks like oak.
THERESA. Oh, I make so many mistakes!
ANGELICA. Well, once you've made a mistake it's best to forget it. You can always rely on friends to remind you.
THERESA. But I haven't any — any stability.
ANGELICA. You don't need stability, dear. Stability is only a virtue if you are a bank, a ship, or a drunk.
THERESA. You just can't believe in anything anymore, can you?
ANGELICA. That's right, dear. You can't even believe what you read in the newspapers — except the obituaries. *(Angelica takes counterfeit bill and puts it in Bozo's topcoat pocket.)*
THERESA. What are you giving it to Bozo for?
ANGELICA. He's papering his apartment.
THERESA. Do you think he's handsome?
ANGELICA. To a goat — yes.
THERESA. Don't you like him?
ANGELICA. If you have a headache, you don't necessarily have to like aspirin.
THERESA. *I* like him. He gooses me. *(She giggles.)*
ANGELICA. Well, that's hardly a valid reason for waxing lyrical, dear.
THERESA. But it's very flattering. Very few nuns get goosed.
ANGELICA. Just don't get carried away before you're carried

away.

THERESA. But there's something terrible I found out about him that I don't know whether or not I should tell you.

ANGELICA. If you mean you've discovered he has a streak of larceny wider than Fifth Avenue, I already know.

THERESA. No. But I found out he's much more naked than meets the eye.

ANGELICA. You've seen him naked!

THERESA. *(Whispers confidentially.)* He wears a toupee. *(Nods.)* He's as bald as a freshly-laid egg.

ANGELICA. Well, if he wears a wig, he probably stole it. But how did you find out?

THERESA. You remember... he asked yesterday if he could take a shower here?

ANGELICA. You looked in the shower?

THERESA. *(Nods negatively.)* He forgot his toupee and left it on the toilet seat. I thought it was a rat and tried to kill it with the broom.

ANGELICA. Did you tell him?

THERESA. Heavens no! I didn't want to embarrass him.

ANGELICA. Darling, nothing would embarrass him except to be told that he was honest. Now, leave me alone for a moment, dear. I'm writing out our monthly check to send to Tania. She gave me a new address in Rome.

THERESA. Don't you think it's strange that we haven't heard from her in so long?

ANGELICA. Maybe there's a mail strike in Italy. They're always striking about something — pollution, prostitution, pasta.

THERESA. I have a funny feeling that something terrible has happened to her.

ANGELICA. Now, what could happen to her that would be so terrible?

THERESA. Well, she might have gotten married.

ANGELICA. That would be a good reason *not* to write. Brides on their honeymoons seldom take fountain pens.

THERESA. Well, even on her honeymoon, she could find time to

send a postal card.
ANGELICA. Not if she married an Italian.
THERESA. Well, it's very odd.
ANGELICA. Why don't you go look out the window — she may have sent a pigeon. Rome is full of pigeons.
BOZO. *(Enters and addresses Theresa.)* Hi there, gorgeous. You back?
THERESA. *(Giggles.)* I guess so. I'm *here*.
BOZO. *(Leers.)* Anybody ever tell you you have a beautiful behind?
THERESA. Everyone. *(She squeals with laughter. Bozo pinches her behind and she squeals even louder. Angelica watches disdainfully.)*
ANGELICA. Commissioner Bozo, may I remind you that we are business partners — not bed partners.
BOZO. It's me hot Spanish blood. By the way, you gave them the wrong address on that dog tag.
ANGELICA. Of course I did. Do you think I want any nosey cop like you coming here to return a lost dog?
BOZO. I think if that dog got lost, Ben would lose his mind. He's nuts about that mutt.
THERESA. And he is, too. They sleep together. I think that's sweet. You have someone to talk to.
ANGELICA. Ben keeps him on a leash and no dog ever wandered off on a leash — which is pretty good advice for wives with husbands who wander.
BEN. *(Enters wiping his hands.)* I wish someone would invent a soap that tastes good.
ANGELICA. *(Counting coins again at the table.)* That's life, Benjamin. You take the bitter and the sweet. That's why the Chinese invented sweet-and-sour pork.
THERESA. *(Sits at table to help count coins. Bozo and Ben join her.)* Anything nice happen to you at medical school this morning, Benjamin?
BEN. Yes. Some rich old maid died and remembered us in her will.
THERESA. That was sweet. What did she leave you?

BEN. Her corpse.
THERESA. I'm sorry I asked.
BOZO. You mean — you mean the one she lived in?
BEN. *(Nods.)* She was over a hundred years old and only weighed seventy pounds. Lying on that marble slab with her clothes off, she looked like a Christmas turkey ready for the oven.
THERESA. Let's talk about something nice — like *flowers*.
BEN. It's interesting about age... if you live to be over a hundred, the body begins to shrink and get brown spots.
BOZO. Yeah, I know — just like a banana.
BEN. This poor old gal's bosoms looked like half-filled leather water bottles.
THERESA. *(Loudly.)* I just love chrysanthemums. But they're awfully messy on the dinner table. The petals fall off and float around in the soup.
BOZO. I had an old bitch dog once — a St. Bernard I called "Slobber," only she had eight tits. They hung in a row like wet socks on a clothes line.
THERESA. *(Louder.)* Pansies are pretty! Violets, too!
BOZO. Do you get many corpses willed to you, Ben, or do you have to steal 'em?
THERESA. *(Even louder.)* Gladiolas are nice. I once had a girlfriend named Gladys. Gladys Gladstone. Isn't that interesting?
ANGELICA. Do *you* operate on these donated corpses, Ben?
BEN. The instructor does. He's cut up more bodies than a chicken farmer.
THERESA. *(Almost shrieking.)* Century plants take a hundred years to bloom. Don't you think that's too long just to smell a blossom?
BEN. *(Ignoring her.)* Another interesting thing. Did you know that every human body has about thirty feet of intestines? Can you picture that?
ANGELICA. Of course. That would measure about one tenth the height of the George Washington monument.
BOZO. I once had a twenty-six foot sailboat. Imagine, my guts

was longer than my boat.

THERESA. *(She stands.)* If you don't change the subject, I'm going to scream, faint, or throw up! Take your choice.

ANGELICA. All right, dear. *(Pats her hand.)* We like Chrysanthemums, too. *(To others.)* She ate a bad oyster. *(Changes subject.)* There's something else I want to talk about anyhow. Since we're all working together, I have some proposals to make for your approval.

BOZO. Such as?

ANGELICA. Well, we've done pretty well for the past few weeks, but we've got to think big.

BEN. How big?

ANGELICA. I suggest that we buy this building.

BOZO. That's big.

BEN. Buy the building?

THERESA. Why should we want a whole building? I can hardly keep the bathroom clean.

BEN. Where would we get the money?

ANGELICA. I'm coming to that.

BOZO. If we own this building, we'd lose our kickback from the landlord.

BEN. What would we use it for?

ANGELICA. Office space. I want to recommend that we go into a respectable business. The lottery racket.

THERESA. The lottery racket?

ANGELICA. It's legal.

BOZO. I don't like the idea of turning legal ... it gets complicated.

ANGELICA. We can be rich and respectable.

THERESA. Can you be both?

BOZO. You mean we'd print and sell our own lottery tickets?

ANGELICA. You're quick, Bozo dear. You've got a mind like a steel trap — with the accent on ste*a*l.

THERESA. And it's legal?

ANGELICA. Of course. States do it, cities do it, and even

churches. There are lotteries to save starving Basutos, the whooping crane, and even the humpback whale.
THERESA. Wouldn't my sister have made a good diplomat?
ANGELICA. What makes you think I'm not? In this country, gambling is as popular as sex.
BOZO. And just as rewarding if you score.
ANGELICA. Well comrades-in-crime, what do you think of the idea?
THERESA. But if we start our own lottery, wouldn't it have to be for a good cause? Like starving pygmies or poor retarded people?
ANGELICA. *(Pats Bozo on the head.)* Bozo's retarded, and our lottery would be for a good cause. We could call it a Campaign to Help the Handicapped. *Us.*
BEN. What if we get investigated?
ANGELICA. Have you ever heard of any lottery ever being investigated? The public has more faith in lottery tickets than they do in the Bible. It's the new way to be saved.
BEN. Who'd sell tickets?
ANGELICA. *We* would. Did you ever hear of anyone who wouldn't buy a lottery ticket from a cop, a nun, or a blind man?
THERESA. Isn't my sister smart? I'm so proud of her. She thinks with her brain.
ANGELICA. And we could hire a few close friends to sell tickets for us, too. I know a couple of Puerto Rican girls up in Harlem who are out of a job. They used to wash dishes at that terrible restaurant where we worked once.
THERESA. The Armpit.
ANGELICA. *(To Theresa.)* You remember them, don't you, dear? Novena Gonzalés and her sister Margorilla.
BEN. Margorilla?
ANGELICA. They were both prostitutes for a while but they repented. So we can trust them.
THERESA. They found God — and food stamps.

ANGELICA. They even have a brother we might use named Retardo.

THERESA. Oh, Angelica honey, people wouldn't buy tickets from *him*. He's a dwarf.

BOZO. Hey, that's terrific. That's better than a three-legged dog.

BEN. How do we know if this building is for sale?

ANGELICA. I checked. We can get it for thirty thousand down.

THERESA. Thirty thousand? Why that's thirty *thousand!*

BOZO. If we're going to rob a bank, Bowery Savings is closest. We won't have to take a taxi.

ANGELICA. We can raise it ourselves. You know that health food store in the next block? Well, it's very unhealthy and going bankrupt. If we can take a lease on it, we can qualify as a small business and get a government loan. We'll take that loan and buy this building instead.

THERESA. God would punish us.

ANGELICA. Darling, God's eye is on the sparrow.

THERESA. Well, there are senators in congress who keep an eye on that sort of thing.

ANGELICA. Those senators set a very good example for us to follow. Mississippi's Chairman of Appropriations got himself an extra hundred million bailout in 1983 alone for his cotton harvesters. And then quietly added another three million. Massachusetts' representative funneled twenty-two and a half million to his favorite Boston college. I'm an economic coward — I'm only asking for thirty thousand.

THERESA. But that's a million.

BOZO. Your sister's right. Life is a rat race. And, if you want to win the race, you gotta be a rat.

BEN. It's going to take a lot of guts.

ANGELICA. All it takes is the right attitude, some Christian fortitude, and a little moral lassitude.

THERESA. Thirty thousand.

BOZO. I like the idea of being landlords. When winter comes, we can raise the rents. People don't like to move in the snow.

ANGELICA. *(Pats Bozo on the head.)* That's what I like about you, Bozo. You're a man of vision .... a veritable vat of venality, vice, venom, and vacuity.

BOZO. *(Beams.)* Gee, thanks. I never know what you mean by what you say, but it don't matter. When you pat a dog on the head, it don't understand either. So, I'll just take it you mean somethin' nice, and wag my tail. All them big words make me feel important.

ANGELICA. Well, as my dear-old-mother always said, "Kindness doesn't cost you anything, so even a pauper can afford to be generous."

THERESA. Thirty thousand!

ANGELICA. I've got even bigger plans. You know that empty church with all the broken windows on the corner that used to be the Ethiopian All Saints Brotherhood Shrine?

BOZO. I never went in.

THERESA. Thirty thousand!

ANGELICA. Stay with us, Theresa — we passed that station. *(Turns back to the others.)* Well, it's for rent, too.

THERESA. Can't we go to church without renting one?

ANGELICA. That can be the *next* business we go into — BINGO.

BEN. Bingo?

ANGELICA. Why not? Everything is a conglomerate nowadays. Movie studios and baby food companies are owned by Standard Oil or DuPont. Spaghetti factories are owned by the Vatican. We're in good company. No one has latched onto BINGO yet as a national industry. This can also make us independent.

THERESA. At least we'd be bringing people back to the church.

ANGELICA. Of course we'd have to change the name of the church. After all, we couldn't call ourselves the Ethiopian Brotherhood.

THERESA. No — we're not Ethiopian.

BOZO. Hey, I got an idea! We could call ourselves the Church of

Christian Converts. "Join and beat the devil."

ANGELICA. That's brilliant, Bozo dear. Why don't you write commercials for Draino? *(Pats Bozo's shoulder and he beams.)*

THERESA. Will we be breaking the law?

ANGELICA. There's no law against religion. *Yet.* And once we're rich, we can make our own laws. That's one of the privileges of affluence.

THERESA. Wouldn't it be wonderful if mother were still alive. We could have her teeth fixed.

BEN. What did she die of, Angelica?

ANGELICA. Embarrassment. When our father deserted us, she couldn't hold a job either.

THERESA. Poor, dear Mama. She taught French in high school for a while until they found out she couldn't speak French ... and fired her.

BEN. What did she do then?

ANGELICA. She did what any sensible woman does when she's been fired. She went home, cried, and took a bath.

THERESA. When we were children, she made our dresses out of old pillowcases.

ANGELICA. When we went to church we looked like walking duffel bags.

THERESA. We went to Negro churches where no one cared. They loved us there. Instead of candy canes for Christmas, those sweet black mothers gave us sugar-tits.

BEN. They gave you *what?*

ANGELICA. It's sugar tied in a rag.

THERESA. We grew up thinking Santa Claus was black.

ANGELICA. And would you believe it. Mother made our underwear out of stolen motel towels. That's how poor we were.

THERESA. How would you like to wear underwear that said "Dew Drop Inn" across your behind?

BOZO. I don't wear any. I get to bed quicker ... among other things.

ANGELICA. With what I have planned, we'll be independent in less than two years.

BOZO. I already been shoppin' around for my old lady's tombstone. She never had nothin' in her life. Except me. Not even an umbrella. *(He begins to weep.)* Well, I'm gonna get her the biggest goddam marble angel you ever seen to stand over her grave. That's the least I can do for her now. *(Looks heavenward.)* Mama, are you listenin'?
THERESA. *We* are.
ANGELICA. *(Pats him again.)* There's a kind of nobility about you, Bozo.
BOZO. *(Sobbing.)* I'm a slob. I can't help it.
THERESA. *(Hands him a handkerchief.)* Here's your handkerchief back.
BEN. Have you found your angel yet?
BOZO. Yeah, I was lucky. There's a dump over on Celestial Street with hundreds of tombstones for sale .... run by a Wop that can't hardly speak good English. He showed me a big eight-foot angel ... bigger tan Mama herself ... only this angel is holding up a marble sword to keep the devil away. Costs five thousand bucks. Made in Japan.
BEN. Isn't that a lot of money to spend on an angel?
BOZO. Are you nuts? I ain't gonna pay nothin'. I found out this Wop owner got into this country illegally. *(Blows his nose noisily.)*
ANGELICA. You're mother will be proud of you, Bozo ... wherever she is. *(The phone rings.)* Will you answer that, Ben? If its an obscene telephone call, say I'll be right there.
BOZO. You get many obscene calls?
ANGELICA. Why do you think I have a telephone?
BEN. *(Into phone.)* Hello. Yes. Hold on. *(To Angelica.)* Some girl in the lobby wants to talk to you.
THERESA. Oh, I hope it's Margorilla. Have we got any rum?
ANGELICA. *(Into phone.)* Hello. Yes ... it is. Who? *Who!*
THERESA. Who?
BOZO. Who?
BEN. You sound like owls.
ANGELICA. *(Puts her hand over phone.)* Oh my God! It's Tania.

(Then back into phone.) What are you doing in the lobby? You're suppose to be in Europe!
THERESA. Tania! That's our neice — Tania.
ANGELICA. *(To Theresa.)* She's in the lobby!
THERESA. That proves she's alive!
ANGELICA. *(Back into phone.)* Tania, darling — what are you doing in America — in the lobby?
BOZO. Everybody wants to come to America. So what's new?
ANGELICA. Well, come right up. We're in B-Flat — I mean Flat B. We can't wait to see you, darling! *(Hangs up.)* Tania! Our own little Tania. We haven't seen her since she was twelve. *(Gasps.)* Oh my God — she can't find us like this — dressed as nuns!
THERESA. *(Wails.)* What will we do? She'll find out about us.
ANGELICA. We've got to get out of these outfits — quick!
BEN. You won't have time.
ANGELICA. We can't let her find out about us — now. She thinks we own a bookstore. *(Starts for bedroom.)* Keep her here for two minutes. We'll change and hide these damn habits.
THERESA. Where do we hide them?
ANGELICA. Under the rug, in the refrigerator. Who cares!
BEN. What'll I tell her?
ANGELICA. Make up anything. We're in bed. In the tub. Think of something! Think of something! *(They lift their skirts and flee into bedroom.)*
BEN. *(To Bozo.)* Think of something!
BOZO. *You* think of something — you're younger. *(Bozo and Ben get on their knees and crawl around the floor picking up coins.)*
BEN. She's bound to wonder why they aren't here to greet her!
BOZO. I got it. We'll start a fistfight. I'll knock you out, and they're in the can gettin' iodine.
BEN. Why don't I knock *you* out — I'm younger. *(The door bell rings.)*
BOZO. Take your time. We're hard of hearin'. *(He freezes on the*

44

floor. Ben rises and walks slowly to the door.)
BEN. I'm lame. *(Waits at door for second ring.)*
BOZO. The doorbell don't ring. Wait'll she knocks.
BEN. She can hear it, stupid. *(Opens door. An attractive young girl enters with suitcases.)* Come in. You must be Tania.
TANIA. Thank you. *(Looks around.)* Where are my aunts?
BEN. Where are they, Bozo?
TANIA. *(Sees Bozo on his knees.)* What's he doing on the floor?
BEN. He lost his Congressional Medal of Honor.
TANIA. But where is my Aunt Angelica? She said come right up.
BEN. Tell her, Bozo.
BOZO. *(Rises.)* Well, it's kinda embarrassing. As a matter of fact, I hadn't oughta tell you. But ya see — it was like this — to call a spade a spade and make a long story short. Ben, here has a dog and they was givin' it a bath in the tub when you called. They was in bathing suits to keep from getting their clothes wet, and they didn't want you to see them that way ... so they run into the bedroom to change.
TANIA. Who's he?
BEN. A genius.
BOZO. So sit yourself down, sister. Make yourself to home. Do you wanna go to the toilet?
TANIA. No thank you.
BOZO. Would you like a hamburger?
TANIA. I ate on the p-p- *(Stutters.)* plane.
BEN. Maybe we ought to introduce ourselves. I'm Benjamin. I'm a medical student. Your aunts let me use their spare room. Knowing a little about medicine, I save them doctor bills sometimes. If you remember, your Aunt Theresa has a nasal drip.
BOZO. And I'm Professor Bozo.
TANIA. Oh? What do you teach, sir?
BEN. *(Quickly.)* Economics.
BOZO. Yeah. I advise your aunts on money matters.
TANIA. Well, would you please advise them that I'm he-he-here?

BEN. Forgive me for noticing, but I see you stutter. I've always warmed to people who stutter — particularly girls. It makes them seem very feminine and vulnerable. *(Grins.)* And it makes me feel protective and masculine.

TANIA. You're very k-k- *(Stutters.)*

BEN. *(Helps.)* Kind?

TANIA. No — considerate. You don't have to help me.

BOZO. That's him. He helps blind men across the street.

TANIA. *(Looks toward door.)* What do you suppose is k-k-keeping them?

BOZO. Maybe they lost a shoehorn. Why don't you show her your dog, Ben?

TANIA. I'd rather see my aunts.

BOZO. Well, speak of the devil — look who's here! *(Angelica and Theresa enter and stop to gasp. They are both attractively dressed.)*

ANGELICA. Tania!

THERESA. Tania! *(They dash to embrace — twisting her back and forth between them.)*

BOZO. That's sweet, ain't it? Makes you think of Easter bunnies.

ANGELICA. Why didn't you cable you were coming? We'd have met you.

THERESA. Dressed.

TANIA. I was afraid you'd cable me n-n-not to come.

ANGELICA. Whatever would we cable that for?

THERESA. Yes — why ever?

TANIA. Well, I m-m-might be in the way.

ANGELICA. Now — how could you possibly be in the way?

TANIA. Well, you have your bookstore to run. I wouldn't want to add to any of your b-b-business problems.

THERESA. Our bookstore?

ANGELICA. Our bookstore? Oh, that! We sold it. We just do charity work now.

BOZO. You got saints for aunts, Miss.

TANIA. Maybe I can help. What do you do? Raise m-m-money for the needy?

ANGELICA. You could put it that way.

THERESA. *(Quickly.)* How did you like France? It must be very French.

TANIA. Well, they do speak French — but otherwise we're about the s-s-same. Inflation and crime. Is there much petty c-c-crime here?

ANGELICA. Here? Darling, you'd think you were in a convent.

BOZO. Yeah — a nunnery.

ANGELICA. I gather you've introduced yourselves?

BEN. Yes — she's met the *Professor* and I explained why you let me use your spare room.

ANGELICA. Oh yes — Ben's mother was a *dear* friend.

THERESA. Armenian.

TANIA. I could sleep on the s-s-sofa.

BEN. *(To Tania.)* Oh I wouldn't want to put you out.

BOZO. I don't think your aunts would want you two to share the same room — at least, not so soon.

THERESA. He sleeps with his dog. You'd think they were honeymooners.

BEN. Well, not quite.

ANGELICA. Darling, there is something I must ask you. Why was it that you didn't write for so long?

TANIA. B-b-because I — well, it's the reason I came back. I wanted to explain. I'm so ashamed of myself for what I've done.

BOZO. You done somethin' bad?

ANGELICA. Are we keeping you, Professor?

BOZO. I don't mind.

ANGELICA. But shouldn't you get back to your college? You've been out of your class too long, haven't you?

BOZO. I guess I'm bein' given the bum's rush. *(Rises.)* Well, I know when I'm not wanted. No one has to kick me in the ass.

ANGELICA. Please — your language!

BOZO. That's all right. He's a medical student and she musta seen a nude model in art class.

ANGELICA. *(Hands Bozo his coat and hat.)* I'm sorry you're in such a rush. But I'd like to talk to you tomorrow. I want to make some necessary changes in my future portfolio.

BOZO. I'll steal the time. *(He goes out.)*

TANIA. What an odd man to be a professor.

ANGELICA. All professors are odd. Too much knowledge makes them eccentric.

THERESA. And bald. They scratch their heads too much.

BEN. Maybe I better leave, too.

TANIA. Would you mind, please — it's rather p-p-personal.

BEN. I'll walk my dog. His girlfriend might have left a message at his favorite telephone pole. *(He goes out.)*

TANIA. He's nice. I like him.

ANGELICA. So do we.

TANIA. How'd you m-m-meet him?

ANGELICA. Oh, he dropped in on us.

THERESA. Right out of the sky.

ANGELICA. Now, what is this awful thing you've done?

TANIA. Wait'll he leaves. I wouldn't want him to see you c-c-crying.

ANGELICA. Why should we cry?

TANIA. You're going to be so d-d-disappointed in me.

THERESA. Oh dear — I hope you haven't killed a Frenchman.

TANIA. No, but I may have killed your f-f-faith in me.

THERESA. I think I'll plant some sweet peas in the window. They can look out at the pigeons.

BEN. *(Returns with dog on leash.)* See you.

ANGELICA. Oh, Ben, will you stop at the supermarket and get some yogurt — the dog seems to love it.

BEN. He does! *(To dog.)* Why didn't you tell me, pal? What flavor?

ANGELICA. Tuna — if they have it.

BEN. You know, people say "it's a dog's life" like it was a put-down. Dogs have great lives — they're cared for, fed, loved, protected, petted, and forgiven anything they do. I wish I were a dog owned by me.

ANGELICA. You're so right, Ben. There'd be more happy marriages if husbands treated their wives like dogs.

BEN. And they don't care if you're rich or poor. *(To dog.)* Well, let's go, buddy. I'll take you down Lexington.

THERESA. Are the stores nicer there?

BEN. No. There're more fire hydrants. *(He goes out with dog.)*

TANIA. Oh, meeting a kind, decent person like him makes me feel like a l-l-leper.

ANGELICA. Nonsense. Now ... tell us what's bothering you. Who have you killed? Anyone we know?

TANIA. It's worse than that. I've d-d-deceived you. You've worked so hard to educate me and I've f-f-failed you. I haven't justified all the money you've spent on me.

THERESA. Don't say that! You're a *fine* artist. *(Points.)* You painted that beautiful picture. That proves you haven't failed. It's a masterpiece.

TANIA. You really like it?

THERESA. We love it.

TANIA. What does it mean to you?

THERESA. Everything. It doesn't have to have a meaning. A rose doesn't — butterflies don't. Why, lots of artists paint pictures of apples.

TANIA. B-b-but, do you understand it?

THERESA. Perfectly.

TANIA. Then w-w-why have you got it hanging upside down?

ANGELICA. Oh, that stupid professor. I told him how to hang it after he cleaned it this morning. *(Straightens picture.)* Is that what's bothering you? You think you've failed as an artist?

TANIA. That's p-p-part of it. I did something I shouldn't have. Something wrong.

THERESA. We all do, sugar. So did Mary Magdalene, and she was forgiven.

TANIA. I took the m-m-money you sent for art supplies and w-w-went skiing in Switzerland instead.

ANGELICA. We didn't know you skied.

TANIA. I don't. That's how I broke my arm.

ANGELICA. You broke your arm!

TANIA. I haven't been able to paint anything for s-s-six months. I was in a Swiss hospital.

ANGELICA. Oh, is that *all* it is. Well, you'll be able to paint again as good as ever when your arm gets better.

THERESA. And if it doesn't, I read of a poor woman with no arms at all who learned to paint with her teeth. It was in "Reader's Digest."

ANGELICA. It's nothing to get discouraged about. We all break laws, promises, and sometimes an arm.

THERESA. And I read of one man who wrote a book with his feet. He typed with his toes.

TANIA. You d-d-don't understand. I no longer w-w-want to be an artist.

ANGELICA. But you've worked so hard.

TANIA. And for what? To indulge myself. To p-p-pamper my ego. Watching those nurses slave at the hospital to be of service made me realize how shallow and selfish m-m-my life was.

ANGELICA. Well, darling, if you don't want to be an artist, that's all right with us.

THERESA. What do you *want* to be?

TANIA. *(Hesitates.)* A nun. *(Angelica and Theresa jump in unison knocking over a vase.)*

ANGELICA and THERESA. A what!

TANIA. A n-n-nun. I knew you'd be d-d-disappointed. But if you could know what motivates those holy women, you'd understand.

ANGELICA. Oh, we *do* understand. Believe me, *we do*. It's just that — well — your talent would be wasted in a convent.

THERESA. And you're too pretty to be a nun. You'd give some poor old priest bad thoughts — and *that's* a sin.

TANIA. I'm getting older and I have to d-d-

THERESA. Decide?

TANIA. No. D-d-d-

ANGELICA. Dedicate?

TANIA. No ... d-d-*do* something really worthwhile to justify my existence.

ANGELICA. Darling, being pretty is enough. Ask any healthy man under thirty.

TANIA. I want to be a b-b-bride — a Bride of the Lord.

THERESA. Benjamin isn't married.

TANIA. I want to connect with p-p-people — to be of service.

THERESA. Why not a telephone operator? They get paid for sitting down. There're very few jobs for sitting nuns.

TANIA. No. I want to serve in a hospital. I want to c-c-comfort the ill ... and give hope to the dying.

ANGELICA. Those are very noble sentiments, Tania. And forgive me for reminding you, but you *do* still stutter a little. I don't think it would make a dying man very happy to be comforted by a stuttering nun.

TANIA. You can't argue me out of it. I wish I could p-p-pay you back all the hard-earned m-m-money you've spent on me — but I can't. All I can give you is my love and my prayers for a long, happy life.

ANGELICA. Don't make it too long. Things haven't been going well lately.

TANIA. And look on the s-s-sunny side. I'll be here where I can see you every day.

ANGELICA. I don't think that would be a good idea, dear. You'd want to bring your friends from the convent, and there are times when I wouldn't want the place cluttered up with nuns.

THERESA. It's cluttered up enough— *(Quickly.)* With a dog.

ANGELICA. Why don't you wait a while, dear? You may not be in the best physical condition to make a decision after your accident.

THERESA. Yes — are you constipated or anything?

TANIA. No — I know w-w-what I want. Now, could I take a shower and change clothes?

ANGELICA. Well, as long as you won't change your mind, you might as well change your clothes. I'll show you your room. *(Picks*

up her suitcases.)
THERESA. Be sure there're no fleas in the tub.
TANIA. *(As they start out.)* You think I'm c-c-crazy, don't you?
ANGELICA. No more than the rest of us. *(They go out. Theresa sits for a moment, biting her lip. She then rises and races over to get her hidden watering can. She puts the spout to her lips and takes a good swig. She hides the can again behind the fern and returns to sit angelically at the table. Angelica re-enters.)* Why should this happen to us! Now of all times.
THERESA. I knew something awful was going to happen when I woke up this morning. I was sleeping upside down.
ANGELICA. She can't stay. We won't have any income.
THERESA. We'll be back on welfare and potato chips.
ANGELICA. We'll never own this building now if she finds out about us.
THERESA. Not to mention the Ethiopian Church.
ANGELICA. We'll *have* to think of some reason to get her back to Europe. *(Paces in deep thought.)*
THERESA. It's sad to love someone and not want them, isn't it? I think that's the way Mother felt about Daddy.
ANGELICA. I know, dear. You can love someone in absentia, in health and sickness, and in bed — but not in your hair.
THERESA. It's too bad she didn't find a husband instead of God.
ANGELICA. What's important is that she doesn't find out about us. Where'd you hide our nun habits?
THERESA. In the refrigerator, like you said.
ANGELICA. When she comes back, throw them out the window.
THERESA. Maybe we could talk her into being a Swiss nun in Switzerland. She could learn to ski.
ANGELICA. She wants to be near us. We'll never make that thirty thousand now. And this building goes out the window.
THERESA. What are we going to do?
ANGELICA. Apply for food stamps.
THERESA. I hate potato chips.

ANGELICA. We've still a little money in the bank. We'll just have to sit on our assets.

THERESA. *(Brightly.)* Maybe we could have her deported?

ANGELICA. *(Still pacing.)* Maybe we could talk her into becoming a Roman nun. The Italians are destitute for nurses. They're always shooting each other.

THERESA. She'd be closer to the Pope.

ANGELICA. And she likes pasta.

THERESA. But she'd have to learn Italian, wouldn't she?

ANGELICA. You don't have to know Italian to give an enema.

THERESA. I told you we'd be punished. Mother's up there telling God what to do.

ANGELICA. Well, there's one consolation — nothing worse can happen. *(The hall door opens and Ben enters. He slumps against the door, head bowed.)*

BEN. Some son-of-a-bitch stole my dog.

ANGELICA. How! How can you steal a dog on a leash?

BEN. I went into the supermarket to get yogurt and tied him to a parking meter. When I came out — he was gone.

THERESA. Did you put a coin in the meter?

ANGELICA. Maybe he just wanted to go back to the pound.

BEN. No — that dog loved me too much to break away. He was stolen.

ANGELICA. But who would steal a dog?

BEN. A blind man — I don't know. I never had a dog before. I loved that mutt.

ANGELICA. Don't worry, Benjamin — we'll get you another.

BEN. It's not the same. That's like saying, "I'll get you a new brother when yours dies."

THERESA. Think of flowers, Benjamin — you'll feel better. But don't think of dogwood — that won't help.

BEN. Well, I'm going back to look for him. Don't wait up for me. I'm going to St. Patrick's first.

THERESA. You think he's *there?*

BEN. I want to light a votive candle to St. Bernard. *(He goes out.)*

THERESA. *Everything* is going wrong for us. I get a counterfeit bill, Tania wants to be a nun, our dog is stolen, and I've got heartburn. I think I'll go to bed until tomorrow.

ANGELICA. Well, we'll just have to cope. That's spelled C-O-P-E. Do you know what that stands for? Courageous-Obstinate-People-Endure. And "endure" is spelled E-N-D-U-R-E .... and that stands for Everything-Nasty-Disappears-Under-Reasonable-Efforts.

THERESA. Is that from the Bible or a fortune cookie?

ANGELICA. From the heart. *(Paces again.)*

ANGELICA. We'll just have to consider this a challenge ... and cope. After all, there's no storm that can't be weathered ... no disease that can't be treated ... no wreck that can't be rescued ... no break that can't be mended ... no ruin that can't be restored. *(She stops at a fern and picks up Theresa's watering can. She continues around the room watering the various plants to Theresa's horror.)* ... no stone that can't be moved ... no blemish that can't be banished ... no war that can't be won ... no puzzle that can't be solved .. no goal that can't be gained ... no beast that can't be tamed ... no fear that can't be conquered ... no void that can't be filled ... and no goose that can't be cooked. In a word ... "cope." *(She has now emptied the watering can in the various flower pots. She notices that Theresa is in tears at the table and crosses to her. Angelica puts her arms around Theresa.)* Don't worry, little flower ... we'll endure somehow. *(Note: When the cardboard holding the flower stems up is moistened, the plants will all begin to wilt visibly.)* There are lots of good jobs that pay good salaries just to sit behind a desk and look intelligent. *(Looks out.)* I wonder what they are?

CURTAIN

ACT III

PLACE — The same.

TIME — A few weeks later.

AT RISE — Theresa, in another housedress, stands at the window looking out through a pair of binoculars. All of the flowerpots in the room still have wilted plants.

THERESA. Tch-tch-tch! Don't they know that God is watching, too! *(After a moment, Angelica enters with a pencil in her mouth and carrying an audit book and a sheaf of bills.)*
ANGELICA. What are you doing now?
THERESA. Watching the neighbors. It's a lot more exciting than T.V. ... except I miss the commercials.
ANGELICA. You like those dumb commercials, for heaven's sake? *(Sits at table.)*
THERESA. They're not dumb. It's fun to watch all those nice dogs running to gobble up their kibble and fat men eating potato chips and car salesmen hitting fenders with their fists and happy mothers taking diapers out of the dryer just as clean as napkins. They're the best part sometimes.
ANGELICA. Well, you can watch the neighbors. I'm going to figure out what we've got left for rent and yogurt next month.
THERESA. *(After a moment.)* They're at it again.
ANGELICA. Who? That woman who bathes her parrot or that man who bathes his wife?
THERESA. That couple across the hall — the ones that go around naked all the time.
ANGELICA. Haven't they found their clothes yet?
THERESA. No — he's still naked but she has on a little apron. I think she's cooking something.

ANGELICA. What makes you think that?

THERESA. She just hit him with the frying pan. *(Brightly.)* Do you think they're married?

ANGELICA. *(Adding figures.)* Well, I don't think they're on their honeymoon or they wouldn't be in the kitchen. What's *he* doing?

THERESA. Pouring catsup on her. I don't think he likes her.

ANGELICA. Well, you better move away from the window, dear. He may take a shot at her and hit you. Three people have been shot in that building since Easter. Two Puerto Ricans and a social worker.

THERESA. It's all right — they've gone out of the room. There must be somebody at the door. *(She puts the binoculars aside and stops to look at her dead plants.)* Oh, my poor little buttercups. They've all gone to Flower Heaven.

ANGELICA. Well, we can't afford new ones, dear.

THERESA. I know — we can't even afford butter.

ANGELICA. And incidentally, where did you get those *awful* plastic flowers? *(Points to vase on wall table.)*

THERESA. They were giving them away at the supermarket with each six cans of shaving cream.

ANGELICA. For heaven's sake, Theresa — we don't use shaving cream!

THERESA. No — but I thought we could use the flowers. They don't wilt. They just get dusty.

ANGELICA. Oh, well — maybe we can sell the shaving cream to Bozo. At a profit. We're running out of money.

THERESA. I know. And that worries me.

ANGELICA. It worries a lot of people. Well, there's nothing we can do as long as Tania stays on. You don't want her to find out about us, do you?

THERESA. Oh no! She'd kill herself. We can't even afford a funeral either. And that reminds me — will we have enough left to buy flowers for mother's grave on Mother's Day? We have to give her *something.*

ANGELICA. We'll steal some nice plastic lilies from another

grave.

THERESA. Again?

ANGELICA. Oh, don't be so negative. *You're* alive. *(Shouts.)* Be happy!

THERESA. *(Winces.)* All right. I'm happy. Do you think Tania suspects anything?

ANGELICA. I don't know. She found Ben's rope in the closet. Scared her to death. She thought it was a coiled snake.

THERESA. She's right. We're a pit of vipers. How'd you explain it?

ANGELICA. Oh, I told her we used it to decorate our Christmas tree.

THERESA. She must think we're eccentric.

ANGELICA. All unmarried women past forty are eccentric. It's a substitute for sex. *(Ponders.)* Although I have to admit, like a substitute for sugar, it leaves a lot to be desired.

THERESA. Could I think about that for awhile?

ANGELICA. Why not — you've got thirty years.

THERESA. *(After a moment.)* It's a good thing I got rid of our nun's outfits, isn't it?

ANGELICA. And that was very clever of you, dear — hanging them up in your room as window curtains. But doesn't it make your room rather dark and dismal?

THERESA. It matches my mood. Where is she, anyhow?

ANGELICA. She went to the park with Benjamin to watch them feed the monkeys.

THERESA. I wonder who's going to feed us?

ANGELICA. Something very good is going to happen very soon.

THERESA. How do you know that?

ANGELICA. I read my horoscope.

THERESA. And you believe it?

ANGELICA. You have to believe in something. Self-delusion is a healthy crutch until you can walk again.

THERESA. What'd your horoscope say?

ANGELICA. It said, "Your financial situation will improve with the full moon. On the tenth, eleventh, and thirteenth do not invest in oil securities or Mexican pesos."

THERESA. Well, at least we can count on one thing. Things can't get worse.

ANGELICA. One of your great virtues, Theresa, is that you're always optimistic. You should have been a nurse for terminal patients.

THERESA. I can't help it. I'm so depressed at not having any money.

ANGELICA. And of course, you're the only one in the world.

THERESA. You know what I was doing this morning that hurt me to do?

ANGELICA. Biting your fingernails?

THERESA. No. I got my old address book out and erased the names of all the people we used to know who've died.

ANGELICA. Did you check the obituaries? You don't want to slight anyone, dear.

THERESA. It's kind of sad, isn't it — to think of all those phones being disconnected.

ANGELICA. It's always sad, sweetheart — to lose your lease, your lease on life, and your zip code. But then, Heaven isn't complicated. That's why it's Heaven.

THERESA. If we only had something to *do!* I'm so tired of looking at myself in the mirror to find myself. All I find are wrinkles.

ANGELICA. Then sit down and play with yourself. Bozo left a deck of crooked cards. Deal yourself a couple of hands of solitaire and you can let yourself win — if you cheat a little and don't catch yourself.

THERESA. I never win at anything.

ANGELICA. That's not true, dear. You won a door prize once at church when you were only seven. Remember?

THERESA. That's right! I won a dozen golf balls. I still have them.

ANGELICA. That's good — we may have to eat them. *(Theresa lays out the cards and starts to sing.)*

THERESA. "Onward Christian soldiers—"
ANGELICA. *(Stops her.)* Theresa, dear, if you're going to sing that song, please get the words right. You've been singing it wrong ever since you were four years old. It's — "Marching as to war" — not "Margie has to walk."
THERESA. Is it?
ANGELICA. Yes — it "is it." Why do you think people stared at you in church? *(Sits beside Theresa to help her play solitaire.)*
THERESA. I thought it was my voice.
ANGELICA. It was — you sing too loud. They heard you. Play your king.
THERESA. Angelica ... what are we going to *do* if Tania stays on and on! It's been five weeks now.
ANGELICA. I can count.
THERESA. We can't get honest jobs. I don't know how to be honest anymore.
ANGELICA. It'll come back to you — like kissing and other bad habits. Play your deuce.
THERESA. Do you think we could be waitresses at the Armpit again?
ANGELICA. With all those drunk sailors pinching our behind? I'd rather die. I've no intention of going to Heaven with bumps on my butt. Play your queen.
THERESA. They wouldn't pinch us if we refused to wear those nasty bunny tails.
ANGELICA. At my age, I'm not about to wear a bunny tail on my gluteus maximus again. I've never understood what's so attractive about a rabbit's behind, anyhow — unless you're another rabbit.
THERESA. Well, one of us has to think of something — and that means you.
ANGELICA. I know. And I'm tired of thinking for two. There are times when thinking for one is too much to think about. Play your ten, stupid!
THERESA. You're mean to me. And I'm really your real sister, really.

ANGELICA. Of course I'm mean to you, dear. You wouldn't want me to be mean to strangers, would you?

THERESA. Well, I'm sensitive. I've got a spastic colon.

ANGELICA. I'll get you an inner tube for Christmas. Play your red six and black seven.

THERESA. Oh, you always have excuses!

ANGELICA. No — I just try to prove there's an answer to everything.

THERESA. It's sad, isn't it, that God gave you the brains and only made me the pretty one. And brains last longer.

ANGELICA. If it will make you happy, dear, I'll trade my brains for your spastic colon. I often think that's where my brains are anyway. Play your ace.

THERESA. Oh, I love you so, Angelica. Don't ever, ever make me think for myself.

ANGELICA. I'll think about it. Now, you see — you won! All by your little self. *(The door opens and Bozo enters.)*

BOZO. I see you're both here.

ANGELICA. That's very observant of you.

BOZO. And lucky — because I got bad news.

THERESA. I don't want to bear it.

BOZO. I been canned.

ANGELICA. You mean — fired?

BOZO. That's right — canned.

ANGELICA. But *why?*

BOZO. The Captain found out I was drivin' a stolen car.

ANGELICA. Your Toyota? You told me you paid for it!

BOZO. I did. I paid a creep to steal it.

ANGELICA. But *you* didn't steal it?

BOZO. I didn't have time.

THERESA. Then you're no thief. The person that stole it stole it.

ANGELICA. Did you tell the Captain that? Did you tell him who the thief really was?

BOZO. Well, I didn't wanna, but he convinced me I should. Him and two other cops.

ANGELICA. Did he believe you?
BOZO. Unfortunately — yes.
ANGELICA. Why unfortunately?
BOZO. They nabbed him right away.
ANGELICA. Well, what's unfortunate about that?
BOZO. He was a cop, too.
ANGELICA. And you had to surrender your badge?
BOZO. Yeah — they took away my badge, the bastards *(Shows it.)* Here it is.
ANGELICA. How do you happen to have it if you gave it up?
BOZO. I stole it back. This badge has been an important part of my life. To me, it's like a Medal of Honor. I'd rather lose my right arm than lose the right to keep it right over my right heart. Right? Right!
ANGELICA. Do you still have your uniform?
BOZO. Well, I didn't go home on the Madison Avenue bus naked.
ANGELICA. Then that's not such bad news. We can still go back into business once Tania leaves. All you need is your uniform and your badge to scare people into the honest sharing of dishonest gains. Excessive profits set a bad example.
BOZO. And what if I'm caught wearing a uniform when I got no business wearing a uniform? What do I say to some lousy cop?
ANGELICA. You say you're only wearing it this once out of respect ... that you're going to your mother's funeral.
BOZO. She died twenty years ago. I'd be a little late, wouldn't I?
ANGELICA. You're Italian — you're still mourning.
BOZO. But we ain't back in business until your goddam niece goes back to goddam Paris and minds her own goddam business.
THERESA. *(Leaps to her feet and waves a reproving finger under Bozo's nose.)* Don't you swear at my niece! I'll report you to the police.
BOZO. Okay — okay. Don't pee in your pants.
THERESA. We worked with nicer people than you at the

Armpit. Smelled better, too.
ANGELICA. *(Shouts.) Calm down!* Let's not start fighting each other. Let's fight what's happened to us.
BOZO. Got any ideas?
ANGELICA. Plenty. All of them bad.
BOZO. Where's Ben? Maybe he's got some bad ideas, too.
THERESA. He's gone to the monkey house.
BOZO. He's got friends there?
ANGELICA. He took Tania there to watch the feeding of the monkeys.
BOZO. Kids that age get dirty ideas from watching monkeys.
THERESA. Worse than watching T.V.
BOZO. He find his dog yet?
ANGELICA. No, but he's found Tania. I'm hoping he can talk her out of becoming a nun.
BOZO. I just want her to go someplace so we can make an honest living again. I'm riding buses now. I ain't been on a bus since I rode to grade school.
ANGELICA. Well, maybe you'll learn more this time. Of course there's always one way to send Tania away.
BOZO. I don't mean knock her off — that's goin' too far. I may be a shit but I'm not that kind of shit.
ANGELICA. We could tell her the truth about ourselves. Of course, we'd never see her again.
THERESA. No! She'd go into one of those monasteries where they give up talking to each other and she'd never speak to us again.
ANGELICA. Monasteries are for men, dear.
BOZO. Yeah — I don't know *no* women who'd give up talkin'.
ANGELICA. But we're not going to do that. Out of desperation we're going to have to look for honest jobs. Jobs where we'll earn what we're paid.
BOZO. Name two.
ANGELICA. I've got last Sunday's paper. We'll just have to see what's available.

THERESA. We grab the *Times* first from across the hall, but we usually put it back. The news usually isn't worth stealing. Too many nice old ladies get raped. *(Angelica gets the paper.)*
BOZO. I'd join the Navy only I get seasick. That's why I gave up my boat. I kept givin' up my lunch.
ANGELICA. *(Distributing sections of the paper.)* Here — let's see what goodies we can find.
BOZO. *(Opens his paper.)* "Open these pages and you open the door to opportunity." It says that here.
ANGELICA. Well, I didn't think *you* said it — it's too erudite.
BOZO. What's "erudite?"
ANGELICA. Perspicacious.
BOZO. What's "perspicacious?"
ANGELICA. Erudite.
BOZO. Must be an echo in here.
ANGELICA. Well — let's open the door to opportunity. Imagination is the salvation of privation. *(Reads.)* "Baby-sitter wanted. Applicant must love animals."
BOZO. That must mean they've got a couple of mean kids or an alligator in the tub. How's this— *(Reads.)* "Companion for elderly matron. Must be willing to travel. Six weeks vacation granted. Private quarters furnished with maid and chauffeur service supplied. Salary starts at twenty thousand with bonuses—"
THERESA. That's for me! That's for me!
BOZO. —"applicant must speak Polish."
THERESA. I think I'll kill myself.
ANGELICA. And that's not for you either, Bozo. You don't even speak good English.
THERESA. Here's a good one for you, Bozo. *(Reads.)* "Horse trainers needed. Excellent opportunity for advancement. Applicant must be willing to sign a four-year contract. Apply Kuwait Consulate." That near Poughkeepsie?
ANGELICA. A few hours. *(Reads.)* "Carpenter wanted. Inside job. Good pay. Must know trim and circular saw work." That might interest you, Theresa. You're always going around in circles.

THERESA. The "good pay" does. But what does this mean? *(Reads.)* "Precision Control Expert experienced in microprocessor controlled memory system."

ANGELICA. It's not for you, dear. You can't even remember what you're trying to remember.

BOZO. *(Reads.)* "Gourmet— *(He says "Gor-met.")* — chef wanted. Experienced in salads." *(Turns page.)* Not for me. I can't even make a bed — much less a salad.

THERESA. Isn't it wonderful? The interesting kinds of jobs out there just for the asking?

ANGELICA. *(Reads.)* "Nurse technician wanted. Expert in hemodialysis." What in God's name is "hemodialysis?"

THERESA. Something nasty, I'm sure — below the navel.

BOZO. Could be someplace in Connecticut.

THERESA. *(Reads.)* "Venders wanted. We supply carts and bagels. Good prospects for advancement."

BOZO. Yeah — up one street and down another.

ANGELICA. *(Reads.)* "Institutional Superintendent wanted. Eighteen thousand to start. Must be experienced in mental therapy and judo." Do you suppose we could apply as a team?

THERESA. Isn't this exciting! It's like finding raisins in a sponge cake.

BOZO. *(Reads.)* "Pilots wanted. Apply Israeli Embassy." *(Turns to them.)* Either of you dames fly?

ANGELICA. Theresa does — on a little Wild Turkey.

BOZO. *(Reads.)* "Enthusiastic, outgoing person with minimum experience in maximum security penitentiary. State covers insurance. Good hours. Good pay. Good food. *(Tosses paper aside.)* And good-bye. Well, let's call some of these people and see what we can land.

ANGELICA. We can't.

BOZO. Why not?

ANGELICA. We haven't got a telephone.

THERESA. They took it out when we didn't pay our bill.

BOZO. *(Rises.)* No sweat. There's a pay booth on the corner. Let's all go down and make some calls.

ANGELICA. Wait'll I get my purse.

THERESA. We might find some coins left in the coin box.

BOZO. No need — I've got a pocket full of slugs. *(They exit. After a moment, the door is flung open and Tania slams it. It is immediately opened again by Ben.)*

TANIA. I told you not to follow me!

BEN. I want to explain.

TANIA. What's Aunt Angelica going to think — seeing you c-c-chase me up the stairs. You heard her yell at you.

BEN. Yes! She yelled, "Run faster, Ben."

TANIA. I don't want to talk to you. Go away! *(She circles the room, ducking behind furniture with Ben following.)*

BEN. What are you getting hysterical about? I only kissed you in the monkey house. I didn't rape you.

TANIA. I'm going to be a nun! Nuns don't k-k-kiss men in public — or anywhere else.

BEN. I saw all those monkeys hugging each other and I couldn't help myself.

TANIA. I don't want to t-t-talk about it! Go away.

BEN. I know you're going to be a nun and I can't stop you. But I'm in love with you and I can't stop that either.

TANIA. Well, at least stop chasing me — I'm tired. *(She sits. He kneels at her feet.)*

BEN. I love you. I love you. I love you.

TANIA. I don't w-w-want you to love me. You don't know anything about me.

BEN. I know I love you. There's nothing else I need to know.

TANIA. *Please* go. You're only m-m-making things worse for me.

BEN. Then let me make them better.

TANIA. There's nothing you can d-d-do for me. Go away.

BEN. I could give you some memories to cherish when you're an old nun. *(He puts his hand on her knee in supplication. She slaps it away.)*

TANIA. Stop groping me! You're not a m-m-monkey. *(She rises and starts circling again.)*

BEN. What are you afraid of? What are you running from?

TANIA. You ... and a lot of things you d-d-don't know about me. *(Stops to face him.)* Ben ... you're a decent young man—

BEN. Not really.

TANIA. With a great future. You deserve the best life has to offer. And I'm n-n-not the best. Please don't be in love with me.

BEN. You want me to stop breathing?

TANIA. You don't know the r-r-real me. I'm rotten. Rotten to the core.

BEN. What are we in — a soap opera?

TANIA. Go. Go and make your place in the world. And when you th-th-think of me — think kindly.

BEN. We *are* in a soap opera! This could last for years.

TANIA. Why do you think I want to become a n-n-nun?

BEN. You said you want to be of service. Well, service me.

TANIA. How little you know of women. How v-v-very, very little. *(She paces again.)*

BEN. Here we go again. Next episode. Will you sit down! You're wearing out the carpet ... and my nerves.

TANIA. When w-w-women give you a reason, that's never the real reason. The reason they give you a reason is to hide their reason.

BEN. Would you say that again? I'm hard to hearing in my left ear.

TANIA. Oh, don't make f-f-fun of me. The reason I want to be a n-n-nun has nothing to do with faith. I want to atone so I can live with myself again.

BEN. Live with me if you want to atone.

TANIA. Sit down, Ben. I'm going to m-m-make you my father confessor.

BEN. I don't want to be your father — I want to be your lover. There's a difference. *(He sits. She continues to pace.)*

TANIA. Why do you think I came back from P-P-Paris at this time?

BEN. I don't know. Maybe there were excursion rates.

TANIA. You're in for a surprise, Ben. I came back because I'm

w-w-wanted in Paris.
BEN. That doesn't surprise me. I want you, too.
TANIA. And do you know why?
BEN. You're sexy.
TANIA. Oh, you're s-s-so innocent. I could almost love you for that.
BEN. Don't let me stop you.
TANIA. No — I don't think I'll tell you after all. I would only b-b-break your heart.
BEN. Look, I'm a medical student. The human body is self-healing. Go ahead — break it. It'll heal.
TANIA. No — one mustn't hurt a bird with a broken wing.
BEN. You know your trouble, pussycat? You go to the wrong movies. Now, what is it you were going to tell me?
TANIA. No, I can't. I can't face the hurt in your face. But I'll tell you what I w-w-*will* do. I'll write it all down for you to read all alone when you're by yourself. Now go.
BEN. Go where? I live here, too — remember?
TANIA. Go l-l-look for your dog. Go and let me put my soul on paper.
BEN. I'll go to the drugstore. I think we could use some Sani-flush. *(Goes to door.)* And a little sanity. *(He goes out. Tania starts to sob. She gets paper and pencil and starts to write. Finishing, she puts her note on the table. She then goes into her bedroom and returns carrying Ben's rope. She opens the hall door and goes out with it. After a moment the door opens again and Ben returns.)* Tania? I forgot my wallet. Tania? All right, don't speak to me. I guess I won't need my wallet. I'm going out and kill myself. *(He goes out. As soon as he leaves his rope taken by Tania is seen to drop from the skylight. A minute later, Tania returns. She places a chair under the rope. She picks up her note and reads it aloud.)*
TANIA. "I can no longer l-l-live with my secret. Forgive me. I love you. The letter will explain why I must take my own life." *(She puts it back and climbs the chair to tie the rope around her neck. Ben enters and faces her room without seeing her.)*
BEN. *(Toward her room.)* Sweetheart, I can't kill myself. You'd be

left all alone. *(Tania tries frantically to tie the rope around her neck before being discovered.)* Baby, you've got some kind of crazy hang-up. You're tied in knots. Relax. I love you. We're in tune. Let's make beautiful music together. I'll be your violin. You can stroke my fiddle. *(She tests the rope.)* The suspense is killing me. Don't jump to silly conclusions. Jump in my arms. I can't live without you. Don't let me lose you. I've lost my dog. That's enough. Do you hear me? All right then, I'll go. *(He turns and sees her.)* Hey! What are you doing with my rope?

TANIA. Go away! Can't you see? I d-d-don't want to live!

BEN. Take that rope off your neck! Take it off — you idiot.

TANIA. Don't you call me names.

BEN. Take it off! *(He shakes her chair.)*

TANIA. Don't do that! I'll hurt myself!

BEN. Take that rope off!

TANIA. It's m-m-my life!

BEN. It's my rope.

TANIA. Why don't you mind your own business — y-y-you no-good do-gooder! *(Unties rope.)* What did you come back for anyhow?

BEN. It's raining. *(Lifts her down and keeps his arms around her.)* Oh, baby — if I'd come back and found you hanging there, I'd have killed myself, too.

TANIA. And it would have been all m-m-my fault. What am I going to do with me?

BEN. Just tell me what's bothering you.

TANIA. I can't. All right, I will. No, I can't.

BEN. *(Points.)* Shall I read that note?

TANIA. No — I d-d-don't want you to know. So I'll tell you. Will you try not to hate me?

BEN. Give me something hard to do.

TANIA. And will you promise n-n-not to tell my aunts?

BEN. *(Lifts a hand.)* On my mother's grave — whoever she was.

TANIA. Very well. *(Gulps.)* I'm a f-f-fraud. I've been painting copies of famous artists for the past four years and selling them as

original paintings.
BEN. *(Digests this.)* You mean — forgeries?
TANIA. Monets, Renoirs, Van Goghs and God knows how many Picassos. I even painted one of Pope Leo the Third by Tintoretto.
BEN. But *why?* Your aunts were sending you money.
TANIA. I never touched it. It's all in a savings bank. But I had to prove I was good. No one would buy my own paintings.
BEN. Oh boy, are your aunts in for a surprise!
TANIA. No! They must never know. You promised on your mother's grave. They'd die of shame.
BEN. Well, I wouldn't go that far.
TANIA. Now you understand why I had to kill myself or become a nun.
BEN. Tania... let me tell your aunts. They'd be so proud to know how successful you were.
TANIA. No. They're such saints themselves. They wouldn't understand.
BEN. Some of our best saints have been former sinners. St. Paul, St. Francis, Mary Magdalene, Judas.
TANIA. No, I'm going to become a nun and repent.
BEN. Marry me and repent.
TANIA. I'm not good enough for you, Ben. You deserve something better.
BEN. Honestly, I don't. I swear to God, I don't.
TANIA. No, Ben — I can only save my soul by saving souls.
BEN. Save mine. Start at home.
TANIA. No. I've made a promise to God.
BEN. Everybody makes promises to God — in hospitals — in courts — on sinking ships. That's who takes up most of God's time. He'll forgive you. It's old hat.
TANIA. But will I forgive myself? Just consider what I've *done!* I've made Monet, Renoir, Van Gogh and Picasso turn over in their graves. I got more money than they did.
BEN. They don't need it in Heaven. Everything's free there. Be a sensible girl — be a doctor's wife.

TANIA. No, Ben. You're a fine man and you're going to be a fine and famous healer for humanity. I would only tarnish the luster of your life. Walk into the sun and forget me, my dear.

BEN. Can we get the hell out of that soap opera? If you don't say you'll marry me, I'm going to rape you right now. Convents don't like pregnant nuns.

TANIA. You lift a finger and I'll jump out that window.

BEN. No — just jump in bed with me. And you can repent for the rest of your life. *(The hall door opens and Angelica, Theresa and Bozo return.)*

BOZO. Hey, guess what? Theresa got herself a job. She's gonna babysit at the Bronx Zoo. They got a baby hippo.

ANGELICA. *(Sees rope.)* What's the rope doing there?

BEN. *(Quickly.) I* put it up again. I was out of practice.

TANIA. No. He's trying to protect me. *(To Ben.)* You're too decent for me to let you do that, dear Lancelot. *(Turns to Angelica.)* Aunt Angelica ... you might as well know. I was about to hang myself.

BEN. You just did.

ANGELICA. You what!

TANIA. I didn't want to live anymore.

ANGELICA. Oh, my God — you found out about us!

THERESA. I told you she'd try to kill herself if she found out. I told you!

ANGELICA. Oh, Tania, we only pretended to be nuns for *your* sake. It was the only way we could send you the money you needed so badly. We couldn't hold jobs. No one wanted us.

THERESA. Except you. We didn't actually *say* we were nuns. We just dressed like nuns to *look* like nuns.

ANGELICA. And we didn't actually steal, dear. We just sat on our little stools and people put pennies in our pots and felt better.

THERESA. And so did we.

ANGELICA. I know how disappointed you must be in us, but can't you forgive us, darling?

THERESA. We're not worth dying for, sweetheart.

ANGELICA. But how did you find out about us?
BEN. You just told her.
TANIA. You pretended to be nuns — to semd me money?
ANGELICA. We wanted you to be a fine artist and have your paintings recognized.
TANIA. Unfortunately ... they are. *(Tania begins to laugh.)*
THERESA. She's hysterical.
BEN. So am I.
ANGELICA. *(Kneels beside Tania.)* We've broken your heart, haven't we?
THERESA. Hit me. Kick me! Slap me! Only don't hate me ... I'll die.
BEN. *(To Tania.)* I told you you'd make them happy.
ANGELICA. We promise to repent if you'll forgive us.
THERESA. Please stop crying. There's no Kleenex.
TANIA. Ben, do we have any smelling salts?
BEN. Why?
TANIA. They may need it. I'm going to tell them the truth about myself.
ANGELICA. We know all about you dear. There's nothing to tell.
BEN. That's what you think.
TANIA. I never needed the money you sent me. I made quite enough from my paintings.
THERESA. We knew you would.
TANIA. By painting forgeries.
ANGELICA. *(Puzzled.)* Forgeries?
THERESA. *(Puzzled also.)* Forgeries?
BOZO. *(Equally puzzled.)* Forgeries?
TANIA. I copied other famous artists and sold them for the real thing. I was a creative criminal. A fraud.
THERESA. You sold them yourself?
TANIA. I had an agent. He had an art gallery ... and connections.
THERESA. But if *you* didn't sell them, he's the crook — not you.

TANIA. But *I* painted them.

THERESA. A lot of crooks sell automobiles they haven't painted. I don't think you did wrong.

TANIA. But I took the money — over ninety thousand dollars.

ALL. *Ninety thousand!*

BOZO. That ain't criminal — that's big business.

TANIA. It's in a Swiss bank. Maybe more.

ALL. *(Together.) More!*

TANIA. That crook of an agent took most of it. But what am I going to do with it? I'm a fraud.

BEN. Join the club. I was a blind man until I saw the light.

THERESA. *(Points to Bozo.)* And he's a defrocked cop.

ANGELICA. You're a genius. Any fool can fool a fool ... but you learned the learned a lesson ... you outwited and outsmarted the smart. You're an artist. A true artist at your craft.

THERESA. Ninety thousand!

ANGELICA. But why did you do it, Tania?

TANIA. Pride in my work. My ego. But I proved I was good to myself. I've painted so many Picassos I can do it with my eyes shut.

ANGELICA. I sometimes think *he* did. But who discovered they were fakes?

TANIA. Mrs. Picasso.

THERESA. Ninety thousand!

TANIA. I just got out of Paris ahead of the gendarmes.

BOZO. *(To Ben.)* What's a "gendarme"?

BEN. A cop.

BOZO. Imagine that! I been a gendarme all my life and didn't know it.

THERESA. Ninety thousand!

ANGELICA. What are you going to do with the money, dear?

TANIA. I thought I might give it to the church.

ALL. *(Scream.) The church!*

TANIA. It's dirty money.

ANGELICA. Don't worry. We won't let you soil your pretty

fingers.
THERESA. *We'll* wash it for you.
TANIA. But what can I do with it?
ANGELICA. Well, since you asked my advice, how would you like to go into business with us?
THERESA. We could open an art gallery and wear pretty dresses.
TANIA. What kind of business?
ANGELICA. Welfare. Our own.
THERESA. They say charity begins at home.
TANIA. Take it — take it all. I couldn't care less.
ANGELICA. We'd like to buy this building for you.
BOZO. As your business advisors.
THERESA. If we're going to buy this building, shoudn't I wash our windows?
TANIA. There's only one thing I want now.
BEN. Me! I'm cheap.
TANIA. I want to paint something good that's my very own. Something that peple will remember.
BOZO. My old lady's tombstone!
TANIA. No. *(Points to her aunts.)* You two.
ANGELICA and THERESA. *(Together.)* Us!
TANIA. As nuns. And who knows, someday I may hang in the Vatican as a tribute to devotion and dedication. Because you're saints.
THERESA. If we're not hanged first.
BOZO. Hey ... we oughtta drink to that — I mean, her paintin' you.
ANGELICA. We don't keep intoxicants in this house.
BOZO. I'll go buy a bottle of champagne from that crook on the corner. I gotta counterfeit twenty dollar bill.
THERESA. I have some white wine. We could toast with that.
ANGELICA. Theresa! Not again!
THERESA. I bought it to celebrate your birthday.
ANGELICA. That's not for eight months.

THERESA. I like to plan ahead.
ANGELICA. All right — where did you hide it this time?
THERESA. I didn't *hide* it. I just stored it in a safe place. *(She picks up the vase and takes the plastic flowers out ... then a bottle of wine.)*
ANGELICA. I hate to say it — but you're really corrupt, Theresa.
THERESA. It's in the blood, I suppose — with a mother that stole potato chips.
ANGELICA. Well, everybody get glasses! *(They go to the cupboard for glasses.)* It was very naughty of you, Theresa, to squander our money on wine.
THERESA. Not really ... I charged it to the landlord.
TANIA. Do you realize what happened since I came back? I've stopped stuttering. It's because I feel secure again. I'm loved again.
ANGELICA. Oh, you sweet child — let me touch you. *(Cups Tania's face in her hands.)* Isn't it wonderful what touch can do? It's a universal language that everyone understands everywhere. If you're in Helsinki or even Mombasa you can touch a cat or a dog, and they'll understand without language.
THERESA. That's a very nice compliment.
ANGELICA. And why do wives say, "Don't touch me!" when they're mad? They know they'll forgive if they're touched. Ben, touch Tania. Bozo, touch Theresa. And you, dear — *(To Tania.)* I'm going to touch you for thirty thousand dollars.
THERESA. *(Loftily.)* That's peanuts.
TANIA. It's worth more. Touch me again.
BOZO. Let's cut out the crap and drink up. You give us the first toast, Sister Annie.
ANGELICA. Very well. *(Lifts glass.)* To love — *(Then adds.)* And a little larceny .... for that's what love is ... stealing someone's heart.
THERESA. To all those beautiful thieves.
TANIA. To art — which I love.
BEN. To the art of survival — which love makes possible.

BOZO. To my two, true loves.
THERESA. Me and Angelica?
BOZO. No ... crime and corruption. *(He pinches Theresa's behind.)*
THERESA. Forgive him Lord. He's really a good boy. He's buying an angel for his mother.
ANGELICA. Let's drink before our wine turns to vinegar. *(Lifts glass.)* Where'd these lovely glasses come from, Theresa?
THERESA. Five-and-dime. I borrowed them when no one was looking.
BOZO. Wait a minute! *(Points to door.)* There's someone out there listenin'!
BEN. I didn't hear anything.
BOZO. *(Puts his finger to his lips for silence.)* The police! They've come after my badge! *(He hands badge to Theresa.)* Well, I ain't givin' it up. Here — hide it!
THERESA. *Where?*
BOZO. I don't care. Swallow it. *(He tiptoes to the door to listen. He then jerks the door open and looks into the hall.)* Oh my God! *(He steps outside. The others wait. He returns leading Ben's dog with a newspaper in his mouth — if possible.)*
BEN. It's Hippocrates!
BOZO. And he brung you a stolen newspaper, too. *(Ben sweeps the dog up into his arms.)*
THERESA. Someone up there in doggie Heaven must love you, Ben.
ANGELICA. More likely, the mother you never knew.
THERESA. Let's give thanks. *(She starts to sing.)* "Onward Christian soldiers.... Margie has to walk...." *(She sees Angelica frown, and corrects herself.)* "marching as to war..."
BOZO. Bottoms up! Down the hatch! *(They all drink. Let's hope the dog will bark.)*

CURTAIN

PROPERTY LIST

ACT ONE

Folding stools (2)
Red pots (2)
Sign "God Loveth A Cheerful Giver"
Bourbon bottle
Books on bookshelves
Sign "It's Later Than You Think"
Cigarettes
Lighter
Stage money
Rope
Masonic button
Abstract painting
Small bag
Telephone
Butcher knife
Handkerchief
Tray and cups
Bible

ACT TWO

Dog and collar
Dark glasses
Leash
White cane
Dog bowl
Large bowl
Briefcase
Banana

Towels (2)
Stage money and coins
Flowers and vase
Tin cup
Suitcases
Watering can
Flowerstand
Fern
Plants (with cardboard-supported stems)

ACT THREE

Binoculars
Audit book and sheaf of bills
Pencil and paper
Police badge
Newspapers
Plastic flowers in vase
Playing cards
Wine glasses

COSTUME LIST

ACT ONE

Two nuns habits (not *any* denomination)
Jumpsuit
Policeman's uniform
Jogging shorts
Tennis shoes
Shirts and trousers (boys)
Card with "13" on it
Apron

ACT TWO

Suit (Ben)
Topcoat (Bozo)
Dress (Tania)
Dress (Angelica)
Dress (Theresa)

ACT THREE

New dress (Angelica)
New dress (Theresa)
New dress (Tania)
New attire (Ben)
Suit (Bozo)

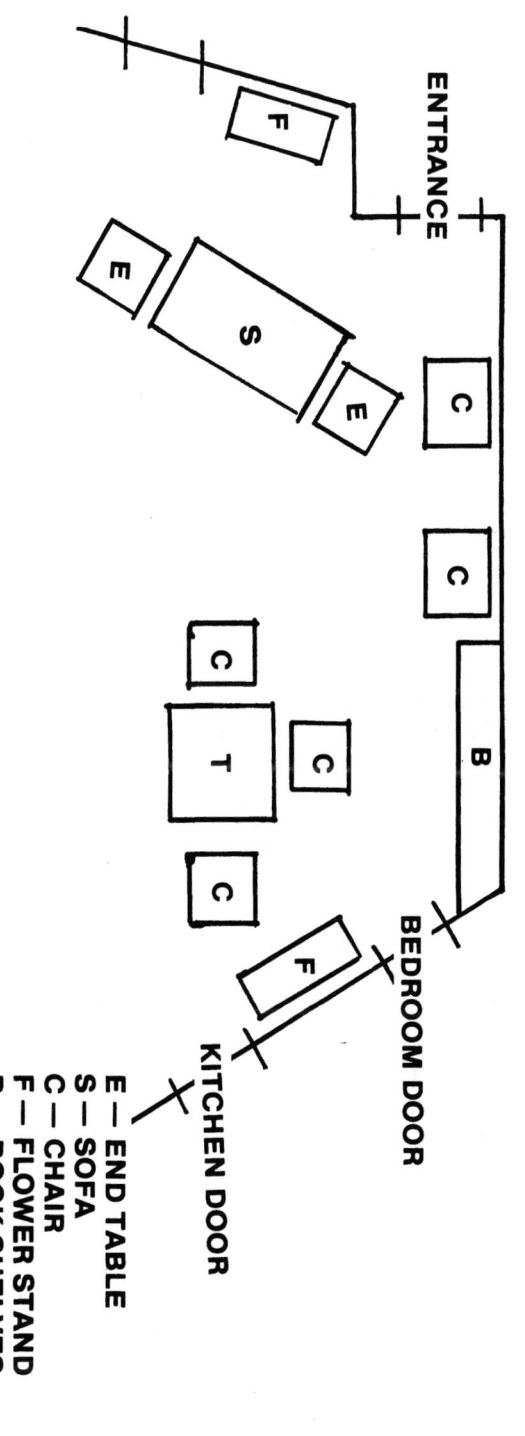

NEW PLAYS

★ **RABBIT HOLE by David Lindsay-Abaire.** Winner of the 2007 Pulitzer Prize. Becca and Howie Corbett have everything a couple could want until a life-shattering accident turns their world upside down. "An intensely emotional examination of grief, laced with wit." –*Variety.* "A transcendent and deeply affecting new play." –*Entertainment Weekly.* "Painstakingly beautiful." –*BackStage.* [2M, 3W] ISBN: 978-0-8222-2154-8

★ **DOUBT, A Parable by John Patrick Shanley.** Winner of the 2005 Pulitzer Prize and Tony Award. Sister Aloysius, a Bronx school principal, takes matters into her own hands when she suspects the young Father Flynn of improper relations with one of the male students. "All the elements come invigoratingly together like clockwork." –*Variety.* "Passionate, exquisite, important, engrossing." –*NY Newsday.* [1M, 3W] ISBN: 978-0-8222-2219-4

★ **THE PILLOWMAN by Martin McDonagh.** In an unnamed totalitarian state, an author of horrific children's stories discovers that someone has been making his stories come true. "A blindingly bright black comedy." –*NY Times.* "McDonagh's least forgiving, bravest play." –*Variety.* "Thoroughly startling and genuinely intimidating." –*Chicago Tribune.* [4M, 5 bit parts (2M, 1W, 1 boy, 1 girl)] ISBN: 978-0-8222-2100-5

★ **GREY GARDENS book by Doug Wright, music by Scott Frankel, lyrics by Michael Korie.** The hilarious and heartbreaking story of Big Edie and Little Edie Bouvier Beale, the eccentric aunt and cousin of Jacqueline Kennedy Onassis, once bright names on the social register who became East Hampton's most notorious recluses. "An experience no passionate theatergoer should miss." –*NY Times.* "A unique and unmissable musical." –*Rolling Stone.* [4M, 3W, 2 girls] ISBN: 978-0-8222-2181-4

★ **THE LITTLE DOG LAUGHED by Douglas Carter Beane.** Mitchell Green could make it big as the hot new leading man in Hollywood if Diane, his agent, could just keep him in the closet. "Devastatingly funny." –*NY Times.* "An out-and-out delight." –*NY Daily News.* "Full of wit and wisdom." –*NY Post.* [2M, 2W] ISBN: 978-0-8222-2226-2

★ **SHINING CITY by Conor McPherson.** A guilt-ridden man reaches out to a therapist after seeing the ghost of his recently deceased wife. "Haunting, inspired and glorious." –*NY Times.* "Simply breathtaking and astonishing." –*Time Out.* "A thoughtful, artful, absorbing new drama." –*Star-Ledger.* [3M, 1W] ISBN: 978-0-8222-2187-6

DRAMATISTS PLAY SERVICE, INC.
440 Park Avenue South, New York, NY 10016 212-683-8960 Fax 212-213-1539
postmaster@dramatists.com www.dramatists.com